The Big Idea

a step-by-step guide to creating effective policy reports

Written by Suri Duitch
Edited by Kathleen McGowan and Carl Vogel
Additional research by Kathleen McGowan, Carl Vogel and Neil Scott Kleiman
Cover & interior design by Julia Reich

THE CENTER FOR AN URBAN FUTURE

ISBN 0-971-86870-0

Library of Congress Cataloging-in-Publication data available upon request.

City Limits Community Information Service, Inc.
Center for an Urban Future
120 Wall Street, 20th Floor
New York, NY 10005
(212) 479-3344
www.nycfuture.org

Executive Director: Kim Nauer
Director: Neil Scott Kleiman
Research Director: Jonathan Bowles
Project Director: David Jason Fischer
Deputy Director: Robin Keegan

Acknowledgements
This book was made possible by a grant from the Annie E. Casey Foundation, which we would like to thank for their financial support, advice—especially Robert Giloth and Susan Gewirtz—and long tradition of supporting the connection between communications and effective advocacy. For their guidance and help, we would also like to thank Gail Nayowith and Rose Anello of Citizens' Committee for Children, Makani Themba Nixon of the Transnational Racial Justice Initiative, Neil Mello of MassINC and Madeline Lee of the New York Foundation.

The Center for an Urban Future is a New York City-based think tank that uses journalistic reporting techniques and traditional policy analysis to produce in-depth reports and workable policy solutions on a range of critical issues now facing our cities.

Contents

Contents

FOREWORD

There is an interesting and often overlooked aspect to the much-hyped information age we live in. Communicating effectively is often a matter of providing less information, not more.

These days, few people—particularly those in positions of influence—have the time to slog through densely-written, poorly organized or ill-argued prose. In the first three paragraphs, people need to know what they're reading and why they're reading it. They need to scan a publication in five minutes and take away all the salient points. And most of all, the information must be reliable and highly relevant to the audience it's aimed at.

Business has known this for decades. Top-flight industry newsletters and trade publications are tightly packed with targeted information and analysis. In the professional political world, the most effective lobbying groups and think tanks spend millions of dollars to produce provocative, lucid research reports and to make sure the right people read them.

You don't need to spend millions to be heard, however. Our secret: employ the research, writing and critical analysis skills that *journalists* routinely use. It's our hope that this book will help you develop your ideas with precision—and sell them with flair. In this day and age, that's a potent combination...and one we bet will work for you.

Kim Nauer and Neil Scott Kleiman
The Center for an Urban Future

CHAPTER ONE

Why Reports Matter

WHY REPORTS MATTER

There's nothing as powerful as a good idea.

And when it comes to changing policy, that's twice as true. With smart writing and recommendations that capture the imagination of the press and policymakers, a few dedicated researchers can help rewrite laws, allocate millions of dollars and most importantly, change people's lives for the better.

Take a report released last November by our organization, the Center for an Urban Future, which outlined how the September 11th terrorist attacks had crippled New York City's world famous arts sector—cutting off ticket sales, donations and government funding throughout the five boroughs. *The New York Times* was interested in the report immediately, running a front page Sunday analysis and, two days later, a favorable editorial. The city's other daily papers and most of the TV and radio stations also began covering the issue. By week's end, the problem was squarely on the public agenda, a major foundation volunteered an immediate $50 million to help ailing arts groups all around the city, and one of the report's simplest recommendations—that students be allowed to resume ticket-generating field trips—was implemented by the city's schools chancellor.

Experienced policy researchers will tell you, however, that most reports end up forgotten, while the problems they were written to address continue unabated. In today's world, faced with an onslaught of information and little time to digest it, people simply ignore much of what comes across their desks. A study that is pedantic, poorly written, hard to navigate or just too long is guaranteed to end up unread, no matter how important the ideas buried within.

Over the last five years, the Center for an Urban Future has written about many topics, including the foster care system,

A study that is pedantic, poorly written, hard to navigate or just too long is guaranteed to end up unread, no matter how important the ideas buried within.

economic development, art and culture, and public education. Few releases change policy in a week, but we have been able to consistently get press, provoke discussion in the field and discuss our ideas with key policymakers. We've learned that getting involved in policy is not just a matter of explaining bright ideas to someone who can make them happen. It also requires strong political skills, good press relations, powerful writing and editing abilities—and a willingness to think critically about your own best efforts.

"People are bombarded with information; they are working

very hard. If you want to be a headline for them, you have to make your stuff available, accessible and attractive, and you have to work it to death," says Gail Nayowith, executive director of the Citizens' Committee for Children in New York.

This handbook isn't a guide to community organizing, designing a web site, lobbying the legislature or creating a new philosophy of political science. It *will* guide you step-by-step to develop and promote substantive policy work in your field, whether your group focuses solely on public policy issues, runs a soup kitchen, fights for affordable housing or protects the environment. With these helpful suggestions, insider's tricks and lessons learned from our organization and groups that do similar work, you'll be prepared to change people's minds and ultimately, change the way things work.

WHO WE ARE

We started the Center for an Urban Future with one simple idea: New York City was in desperate need of a policy group that was keyed in to local problems, could debunk some clichés about urban life, and had the investigative reporting talent to look bluntly at the city's needs and its potential. We had been running a well-respected urban affairs magazine, *City Limits*, for 20 years, and we thought we knew everything about digging up interesting ideas and delivering them to a wider audience. We thought it would be easy. As it turns out, it wasn't—we learned a lot about the pitfalls of the trade, everything from working with other groups to getting reporters to publish our findings.

Throughout all those early trials, we thought a lot about what we were trying to accomplish. One model was conservative think tanks such as the Manhattan Institute and the Heritage Foundation, which grew to prominence in the 1990s by using aggressive reporting and vivid rhetorical arguments. Their writing was crisp, simple and, most of all, engaging. Sometimes they stretched the truth, but they were definitely effective.

Looking around on the left, we couldn't find a similar collection of skills. We did discover groups around the country that do some of what we were aiming to accomplish—from collecting data on health insurance applications in low-income communities to reporting on electricity use in the Pacific Northwest. By taking a page or two from these organizations and using our journalism background, we aimed to regularly produce effective policy recommendations that focus on equity while avoiding ideology.

When we began to find our way, it wasn't because the Center was incredibly well-financed or could call on a long list of powerful allies. On the contrary, our budget was (and remains) relatively small and, to be honest, we were relatively unknown when we opened up shop. Lots of money is certainly helpful, but it isn't required. We've had success because we've tried to create materials and agendas that are well-researched and engaging.

THE SYSTEM

To think about our process of researching, writing and releasing a report, picture that classic hourglass. A lot of work goes in at the beginning to expand your thinking far beyond first impressions; in the middle the topic and focus gets narrowed down; and you try to push the findings far and wide at the

HOT TIP

Expand Your Rolodex

Learning about a range of perspectives on your topic enriches your discussion, helps you evaluate all the options, improves the strength of your position and makes your message smarter and more credible. *Expand your horizons; it will improve your arguments and your writing.*

end. As you begin to work on creating your own agenda, keep these basic steps in mind.

The Research

At the start of the process, you gather information from as many sources as you can, getting data, opinions and ideas from other research reports, newspaper articles and especially from knowledgeable people. You do a lot of work in the beginning, but it does pay off. You'll find ideas and examples that make your report and recommendations both convincing and interesting to read. And after you've developed your agenda, you'll be prepared to advocate for it—because you assembled stellar facts, data and resources at the outset.

The Writing

In the next phase, your understanding of the issue becomes more sophisticated. You and your colleagues decide what is the most important problem in your area and what needs to be done about it. In the process, you narrow all that information down into a simple, clean, easy-to-understand agenda–the narrow part of the hourglass. This gets boiled down even further, into a couple of pithy, easy-to-understand sentences that get your message across quickly. By the time your report has been written, rewritten and edited, it will be a well-honed assessment of a problem and what can be done to fix it.

The Sell

At the end, you are ready to use your agenda to influence the way people think, spreading your proposals as widely as possible. The goal is to advance the public discussion, add new information and ideas, and sow the seeds for real change. What is the obvious problem everyone is ignoring? Why have previous efforts to solve this issue failed? Who can make your recommendations work? You'll have the answers and be able to get them to people who can make a difference.

That's it—that's our basic recipe. Some of what we're going to tell you throughout this booklet is old (but important) news—for example, that you need to plan out your work before you do it, and that getting the press to pay attention is crucial. But some of the things we suggest will probably sound a bit surprising. They may even rankle a bit. But if you read on and suspend your convictions about the best way to reach people and the best way to do policy work, our recommendations can make your work a lot more powerful.

THE TOOLS TO MAKE IT WORK

Any chef will tell you that creating a great meal goes beyond what's listed in the recipe—it takes a skilled hand, fresh ingredients, the right tools in the kitchen. And to be really successful in using our recommendations, you need to not only follow our basic recipe for creating reports, you

INFORMATION

Independent Means

The Center for an Urban Future has been successful in part because we're independent and our ideas don't arrive with predictable baggage. Your group might not have that advantage—if you're an adoption agency, of course your report will be pro-adoption, a union would be expected to call for more protection for workers, etc. But you can still be effective in changing policy and this book can still be a useful tool in reaching that goal. In today's world, nobody expects a report's author to have no agenda. If your findings are backed up by legitimate data and compelling anecdotes, and if you present arguments that are clear and well-considered, your final report can and will get people's attention.

Starting as a player in the field you're researching doesn't absolve you from listening to the other side, however. In fact, it makes it even more important. You're probably quite familiar with how your allies feel about your issue. But you may not have a good understanding of how the press and general public see things—and they're the ones you need to convince. If you don't insert your ideas into the current mainstream view—regardless of whether you like the terms of the debate or not—then you *will* be seen as hopelessly partisan. And your report is almost guaranteed to be ignored.

need to understand some of the underlying philosophies that created it.

Think Like a Journalist

We've found that the most effective way to research, develop and communicate a public policy agenda is to think and act like a reporter. In fact, we consider this idea our secret weapon.

What does "think like a reporter" mean? Well, for one thing, you must be willing to chase down all sorts of leads to get to the facts and new perspectives on the issue, understanding that useful information and new allies can be found in some unlikely places. You have to have a nose for good sources: people who are thoughtful, experienced and more interested in telling the truth than advancing an agenda.

To get the information you need, you also need to be able to work with good sources and gain their trust and respect. Mostly, that works by listening. *If you listen carefully and thoroughly, people respond.* Most people enjoy being asked about their opinions, so take advantage of the opportunity.

We also suggest trying to write like a journalist. If you want to reach people, you need to write well and in an interesting and engaging way. Good journalistic writing is crisp and convincing. It puts complex ideas into simple words. We recommend it.

The one major difference between public policy work and journalism is that journalists try to be objective. You don't have to give both sides of the story—you have a message to convey. But in the beginning stages of research, you should keep that reporter's truism in mind: Work to be as objective as possible. Stay open to learning new things and looking at the issues from different perspectives. Keep an ear open to the controversies, the areas where intelligent, reasonable people disagree.

Be Open-Minded

At the risk of overstating it: *The ability to think critically while developing a sound policy agenda is probably the one thing that will distinguish you from every other group with a good idea and some press contacts.*

The most important word in that overstatement is "critically." A lot of people in the policy world are intelligent—heck, most are. But most are also pretty hidebound to their point of view. If you're willing to get beyond your current thinking on a topic, you can come up with some truly innovative ideas that have a real chance of becoming a reality.

Our definition of critical thinking includes:

- Understanding the historical, political and social context.
- Identifying both the most influential and the most innovative thinkers (not necessarily the same people) in the field. You don't have to agree with them. If you reject their thinking, though, you should know why—and be able to justify it.
- Conducting original research that uncovers new sources of information and new ideas.
- Having a willingness to abandon failed responses to the problem.
- Honestly critiquing your own ideas and proposals, and, more importantly, letting people who don't agree with you critique them to make them stronger.
- Allowing your beliefs and positions to evolve.

On paper, it all seems pretty straightforward, even easy. But how will you react when someone says that welfare reform has been a surprising success? For your report about cleaning up the Hudson River, are you willing to sit down and really listen to a General Electric spokesperson? If you're a housing activist, will you let a university professor who advocates phasing out public housing give you feedback on your first draft?

We're not asking you to hew the corporate line on pollution or to support shredding the social safety net. But your goal is not to parrot a list of well-worn policies. Those are the means. You're trying to find the best way to get to the end: fixing whatever problem you've set your sights on. And if some thinking from the "opposition" or other unconventional sources can be used to advance your agenda, don't ignore it.

HOT TIP

In Other Words

The method that we've developed over the last five years can be summarized in a few basic principles.

- **Think Like A Journalist:** Be skeptical, not cynical; gather an enormous amount of information; don't make up your mind until you have all the facts; listen to all sides of the issue—and once you've chosen your agenda, promote it to the hilt.
- **Find Uncommon Bedfellows:** Groups with different ideologies or goals often are your best allies. It makes your message more powerful. It also surprises people, and makes it hard to pigeonhole or ignore your work.
- **Tell Me Something I Don't Already Know:** If you want people to listen, tell them a story they haven't heard before, or introduce them to a situation or question they don't know about. Better yet, point out new solutions to the problem that everyone else has given up on or assumes can't be solved.
- **Know Yourself, and Know Your Enemies:** Be realistic about what you or your group can accomplish; understand your opposition, their tactics and their weaknesses.
- **Speak Clearly:** Write like a reporter, not a professor. You're trying to claim people's attention—most aren't experts in your topic and all of them are pressed for time. Make it easy for them to grasp your ideas.

When you develop your position, you'll have gathered information from as many sources as possible and carefully analyzed them to come out with something that incorporates the best of what you have learned and is nuanced and clear. Knowing why you rejected other viewpoints or solutions, you'll be able to defend your decision.

Stand Out From the Crowd

A lot of policy writing is boring, ponderous, unfocused or worst of all, shrill. Even if the author has an interesting agenda and point of view, and even if the research is compelling, it gets buried in poor design, too much information, overblown rhetoric or bad writing. *Respect your readers. They shouldn't have to wade through confusing language to understand your message.* One recent policy report, for example, pointed out the need for "reforming existing investment streams to maximize positive neighborhood economic impacts." Huh? What they meant to say—and should have—is simply that money should not be wasted.

To really get your ideas to take flight, you need a broad audience. Without being cynical or dishonest, find ways to appeal to the collective imagination so that your words resonate. "Speak American," as they used to say. Learn how to package your policy goals in catchy language, using current terms and themes and concepts already floating around in the public realm. If you do, reporters and interested citizens will bother to read your report. And policymakers will not only read it (remember, they have even *more* unread reports and papers on their desks than the rest of us), they'll be able to directly appropriate your concepts into their own policy goals and political agendas.

AND BEYOND

So far, we've been talking more or less in the abstract about underlying concepts. But from here on in, we'll go through each stage of the process, giving specific recommendations and examples to illustrate our points. This slim volume can't cover every contingency and skill. We'll focus on what you should be thinking about and give tips for getting it done, but keep an eye out for the Resource boxes to get more help on everything from researching on the web to writing a press release.

While you're doing all this work, keep in mind that your goal goes beyond simply getting mentioned on the news. When you're releasing a report, contacting reporters and holding seminars, you're both changing the debate on a single topic and building your reputation. Rebuilding public policy is a long-term effort, and part of what you're doing is putting your issues on the map and establishing an identity and a role for your group.

"We will spend six months to a year—sometimes over a year—to keep promoting our products and get our findings out there," says Neil Mello, director of external affairs at MassINC, a nonpartisan organization working to build a strong middle class in Massachusetts. "It's not an intensive one-day effort. Just because you released a report doesn't mean that it has sunk in, or that people have been persuaded and are talking up your issue and findings. You're not part of the buzz after being in one news cycle."

After your first project, you'll probably find that people know a lot more about your group and what you do. You'll have a lot of new contacts. Plus, you can spin off other reports, stories and fact sheets from the major project, since you've already done the research and know who you want to talk to and what you want to say.

Regardless of your group's mission, policy work should be a part of your long-term vision for the future. Even if policy is only a sideline to your core mission, it can bring exposure and public recognition to your group. That, in turn, will help you get what you need from policymakers, funders, politicians, regular people and the press. And, of course, if done right, it can help change the world.

CHAPTER TWO

Getting Prepared

Getting Prepared

Before you start reporting, you probably need to do some groundwork. Talk to people informally about the issue and track it in newspapers, magazines and on TV for several months. Don't just listen for what's new (although that's important too). Hear how the issue is generally portrayed and keep track of who is quoted on the topic. This early research also helps you identify your most promising partners and gives you an idea if they're effective, aggressive, convincing, well-connected, etc.

At the Neighborhood Family Services Coalition, a New York City umbrella organization for groups that help families and children, staff director Michelle Yanche puts together a monthly press packet for the members. She includes all relevant articles from the city's newspapers and newsweeklies, whether they are about her member groups, a new judge in Family Court or an important budget decision. If her organization or its members are quoted or interviewed, that goes in the packet too. "The reality is that the media is a really important communication vehicle for us," she says. You may or may not want to start such a formal process, but whatever your style, give yourself some time to really notice how your topic is perceived in the mainstream.

KNOW YOUR ORGANIZATION

It may seem obvious, but *make sure you know what your group is and does before you get going on your agenda.*

If you don't, you can miscalculate the level of support you'll get from your organization. Think tanks come in all sorts of sizes, and you don't have to be a multi-million dollar organization to produce cogent, effective policy recommendations. But you can't conduct a three-year environmental study of five different cities on a $10,000 grant, either. Get a realistic idea of how much time, money and support you can ask for, and scale your project within these boundaries.

Get a realistic idea of how much time, money and support you can ask for, and scale your project within these boundaries.

You may also want to consider other organizational issues. For example, if your group has never done any advocacy before, make sure your executive director and board of directors are aware of your work before you start issuing a series of recommendations—especially if those suggestions are more than the usual bromides on the subject. And think about who on your staff can lend a hand once you begin, both in terms of time and skills.

MONEY CAN BUY YOU...

There's a long list of ways to spend your organization's money

WORKSHEET

Are You Ready?

Before your organization takes on a public policy campaign ask yourself about:

- **Its History:** Has your organization ever worked on public policy issues? Has it ever failed?
- **The Board of Directors:** Who are the board members and why were they chosen? What do they do for a living—businesspeople, philanthropists, activists, pastors? Are they active in party politics?
- **Your Resources:** Do you have cash and staff time? What will your funders think, and do you care?
- **Organizational Culture:** Does your staff like a challenge, and are they willing to invest a little extra energy?
- **Mission:** What is your organization's mission? Is it visionary or is it concrete?

on a policy report. You certainly don't have to come up with cash for all of them. Below we've given an idea of what it might cost you to hire someone to do every single stage of creating a report. Where appropriate, we've given an estimate of prices in New York City, but you may be able to get these services cheaper. Use our list to figure out which assets you already have, which you can beg or borrow, which ones you'll have to pay for—and which you might have to do without. They should also give you an idea of what kind of budget you might want to present in a grant proposal.

We can't tell you exactly what you need and don't: It really depends on factors like the kind of research you need to do, whether you want to send the final product to a hundred people or a thousand, if it will be part of a larger campaign, etc. But we do suggest that you don't skimp on the basics—research, writing, editing and design—whether you do the work in-house or with freelancers.

✓ Staff or consultants with these skills:
- Journalistic experience in reporting and writing *($30-$75/hr)*
- Editing *($15-$40/hr)*
- Graphic design *($35-$60/hr)*
- Database management and other tech skills *($20-$40/hr)*
- Web site design and maintenance *($40-$150/hr)*

✓ A database program like Microsoft Access *($325, or free with some Microsoft office packages)*

✓ Internet and email access *(Free - $20/month)*

✓ A Web domain name *($30-$50/year)*

✓ Local and long distance telephone costs

✓ Travel costs for site visits—consider whether it's local, statewide or out-of-state

✓ A graphic design program like Quark, if you do the design yourself *($850)*

✓ Printing and publication costs *(about $3,800 to print a 16-page, 4,000-copy booklet in black and white)*

✓ Postage and envelopes

✓ For larger distribution: a mailing house to send materials *($250 - $1,250 or more)*

At the Center we generally do the writing, reporting, database management and project supervision ourselves and bring in consultants for the rest of the tasks. We know what we do best, and we hire professionals to ensure the rest of the work is done well and on-time. That said, we don't pay our staff members or our consultants anywhere near what they could get elsewhere. *People are attracted to the work despite the middling pay because it is flexible, interesting and meaningful.* Another tip: where possible, pay freelancers on a project basis, instead of hourly. That way, you don't flinch about the cost every time you ask for a rewrite. For more on who can do the work, see "Putting Together Your Team" on page 35.

One last thought. Don't worry too much if you're not an expert at everything you set out to do in-house. We learned many of our skills on the job. We started a website with less than a thousand dollars. It wasn't much to look at, but it showed enough potential that after a few years we were able to raise tens of thousands of dollars to redesign it. And if you have the skills yourself—and are willing to put the time in—you can teach other smart people on staff to research, write, edit and do press work.

DATABASE DOS AND DON'TS

A database of contacts is one of your most important tools. We are obsessive about this database stuff. *Policy is all about communication, and when you don't know who to reach or how to reach them, you've lost the game before you've even started.* Keeping a clean, current database is a pain in the neck, and can easily fall by the wayside. Unfortunately, that is usually just about the time that you find out your opponents are organizing

INFORMATION

What's Your Bandwidth?

For proof of the power of technology, look to the protesters that derailed the Seattle World Trade Organization meetings in 1999. How did this loosely organized, inexperienced band of teens and 20-somethings coordinate a massive international demonstration in a matter of months, including a savvy press campaign? Over the Internet. "From the very beginning, we used listservs and email to communicate," Rainforest Action Network's communication director Mark Westlund told the *San Francisco Examiner* in 1999. "We had the broadest coalition of groups that I have ever seen come together on one issue. They were all communicating via the Internet."

Most people in public interest work and nonprofits haven't kept up with technology. Being cash-poor isn't really an excuse anymore. These days, even the cheapest computers come with modems, and Internet access and email accounts can be had for free. Getting proper training in using these new technologies can be more complicated, but some local groups offer cheap or free classes to nonprofits.

No question, your work will improve as you learn to conduct web research, and it's a lot faster to find useful documents and publications via the Internet than taking a trip to the library. While there is a lot of junk out there, there are also goldmines of information. (See page 59 for a few of our favorites.) Your writing improves as you write email, and you can communicate with even local colleagues much more efficiently. And when it comes to wide information dissemination, it usually is much cheaper.

For some additional thoughts on creating a technology-proficient organization, see "Seven Characteristics of an Online Organization" by One Northwest (onenw.org/toolkit/modestproposal.html). Another good resource: The Benton Foundation's site (benton.org), which has up-to-date information on Internet advocacy and communications.

a big turnout for an important City Council hearing next week.

At MassINC in Boston, keeping a broad, carefully maintained database has paid enormous dividends, says Neil Mello. "Personally going through files and making judgements about who's in the database matters a lot. For example, one day we noticed we had no information on Andy Card." Card, now the

HOT TIP

To Get Technical

It doesn't take much to get the technology you need to create a report. Your necessary basics to join the communication age:

- An up-to-date database with all your contacts.
- Internet and email access. Free services at the end of 2001 included netzero.com or bluelight.com.
- A working website, with your mission statement, contact information and policy areas.
- A basic understanding of Internet research techniques. If you need training, try your local library.

Chief of Staff for President Bush, had once been a prominent Massachusetts GOP figure, but he had left the state to pursue opportunities in Washington. "Even though MassINC's primary focus is on influencing leaders in Massachusetts, we still thought it worth the effort to track down his current mailing info, and keep sending him our stuff."

That diligence paid off in an unlikely way when the group was trying to make inroads with Republican Governor Paul Cellucci's administration. "As a nonpartisan policy group, we continually need to earn the confidence of leaders in both parties in Massachusetts, and we weren't quite there yet with the Governor," Mello says. "Now it just so happened that shortly after we began sending him free copies of our magazine *CommonWealth*, Andy Card decided to talk about the magazine at a dinner with the Governor and his staff in Washington. Apparently he had very nice things to say, and that probably had a positive influence on how the Governor and his staff came to think about the work MassINC does. We're certainly glad we took the time to update his file." Since then, MassINC's relationship with the administration has prospered.

So just who is going into this database you're building? It should include every single person you can think of who is interested, or who you want to interest, in the subject and in your work. (As you do your reporting, you'll keep adding names.) Your database should include:

- People who you've interviewed
- The people most directly affected by the issue
- Government employees who work on this issue
- People who have attended conferences and forums on the topic or on a related topic
- Academics
- Foundation executives and other charitable donors
- Reporters and editorial page editors
- Elected and appointed public officials

Please note that people actually do respect you more for spelling their names correctly and using correct addresses. It improves the way they think about your organization. Make sure to include email addresses, too. Emailing is the easiest and fastest way to communicate these days, and the list will come in handy later when you are about to release a report.

"Databases are vital, and they *must* be done in-house," Mello says. "We have a staff of 12, and we have three full-time professionals working on databases in-house. The head of our database unit has two advanced degrees. Database work is very labor intensive and it is mundane. It is easy to farm it out and have a temp or an intern do it. We think this is the wrong move. The thing to bear in mind with databases is that quality counts much more than quantity."

You might not have a scholar in charge of your database, but the keeper needs to have a nose for who to add, who to track down when they switch jobs, and who not to bother with. In some ways maintaining a good database is like being a good reporter—following the people in your beat and having a sense of who needs to be getting your reports.

CHAPTER THREE

Building an Agenda

Building an Agenda

You probably already know what issue you want to explore, but you need to choose a fairly tight focus. It's hard enough to change a specific policy—it's pretty much impossible to shift the entire issue landscape in one fell swoop. You might feel that the American economic system is stacked against the poor, but you're more likely to make a difference if you start with something like shortcomings in local job-training programs for the unemployed.

"The ideal thing for an activist to do is come up with the issue that is winnable and gets to the heart of the beast at the same time," says Robert Gangi, executive director of the 157-year-old Correctional Association of New York, an advocacy group

You should consider if you essentially agree or disagree with most of the groups working on your issue. Are you going to have a lot of allies or foes?

that works on criminal justice and prison reform. That's a huge subject, so they have focused on a few specific issues: monitoring conditions in state prisons, pressing for more humane treatment of female prisoners, and (especially) working to change New York State's expensive and draconian Rockefeller drug laws.

Gangi says the drug law campaign is a perfect example of how his group tries to carefully balance the practical and the

WORKSHEET

How Should We Attack This Issue?

When considering exactly what aspect of the issue you want to investigate, ask yourself the following questions:

- What is the problem? What is the policy that is causing it or making it worse?
- What is most pressing about the situation?
- Do I know of any logical, moral, economic or administrative problems in the current situation that are easily explained?
- How much time do I have to devote to this issue?
- What resources do I have, and how much work can they support?
- What is the political climate of this issue? Are there any politicians who will be interested in my approach?

Now think about what those answers might mean to effective policy recommendations. As you can gather from our questions, the chances of making a difference can be affected by how big your problem is, how simply it can be solved, who gains—politically or financially—from it being left alone, etc. If you think through these factors, you're much more likely to be able to make a difference.

RESOURCES

Useful Theories of Social Change

As you think about a specific topic to research, you may want to consider how ideas catch people's imagination. Two recent books present intriguing and easy-to-digest models on how a dance craze, product, idea or policy gets in everybody's head. "The Tipping Point" by *The New Yorker*'s Malcolm Gladwell uses the model of an epidemic to explain how change often begins suddenly, in response to apparently insignificant events.

"Unleashing the Idea Virus" by Seth Godin is more of a business tome, but his clever examples and underlying thesis give readers a primer on how to catch people's attention—and how to get them to pass your ideas along. An overview of Godin's work can be found at www.fastcompany.com/online/37/ideavirus.html. The entire text of his book can be downloaded for free with a link at the end of the article.

visionary: "You can mobilize people that care about prison issues as well as those that care about government priorities. You can make points about it in pretty simple ways and build simple coalitions. You can talk about the laws being wasteful and ineffective, and you can also point out that those laws are racist and morally perverse. You make all the arguments because that's the fair thing to do, and because you stand a better chance of reaching more people." *In other words, the issue isn't only important, it's also winnable.*

KNOW YOUR COMPETITION...

Once you've been listening to the news and have started a good database, you should begin to analyze just who else is working on the policy you're eyeing. There are no real wrong answers here. But you do need to take the landscape into account.

For example: Are you entering a loud, messy debate? That can be daunting, but it doesn't have to end your campaign before it begins. When we started a biannual report on New York City's Byzantine foster care system, some allies warned that sharply partisan politics, lurid abuse cases and the self-interest of nonprofits with city contracts left no breathing room for any new ideas. But we found that by being very clear about which parts of the system we were critiquing—and by emphasizing our independent role—we actually provided a refuge. A lot of people who cared very much about making the system work for both parents and children had been trapped by overwrought rhetoric and inflexible positions. Your case might be very different: Maybe you need to shake things up, rather than cool them down. The point is, every issue has players and battle lines. Figure out where you might fit in.

You should also consider if you essentially agree or disagree with most of the groups working on your issue. Are you going to have a lot of allies or is it you against the world? Size up the people who don't agree with you. Think, for example, of what it means if your opponents give massive campaign contributions. Knowing that will certainly help you decide which politicians to approach and which not to waste your time with. Do they get access to policymakers, politicians and the editorial boards of local newspapers through money (advertising, political contributions, etc.) or relationships (hiring lobbyists with connections, having gone to the right schools and joined the right clubs)? Again, these answers shouldn't convince you to simply quit the battle altogether—but they should help you decide how to fight.

... AND PICK YOUR PARTNERS WELL

Collaborations are essential to this process. You're attacking a huge problem with a small band of researchers and a fax machine—you need some allies.

You'd be surprised what you can accomplish when you're willing to go beyond the usual suspects. Say you're working on a campaign to change a truck route in your neighborhood. Collaborators could be the leaders of the local PTA who are worried about kids crossing busy streets, a transit expert at the local university or clean-air activists.

Make sure that you aren't just talking to people who think the way you do. That's one of the worst, and easiest, mistakes to make.

When President George W. Bush announced that he intended to repeal the estate tax at the beginning of 2001, nonprofits were horrified. To avoid the tax, wealthy people donate millions of dollars each year to nonprofit causes, and without those donations, many organizations would not survive. The people at United for a Fair Economy, a group that fights income inequality, reached out to prominent philanthropists like George Soros, the Rockefellers and Ted Turner, and together they launched a high-profile campaign against the repeal. People were startled that multi-billionaires, who had a lot to gain from the tax cut, were willing to take a principled stand against it. The tax cut was ultimately passed, but in a more moderate version—thanks in part to the lobbying efforts.

Keep in mind that you want some of your collaborators to do more than stand on the podium at your press conferences. You're looking for people to test your ideas and to help you refine your message. Every conversation that you have and every perspective you integrate will help improve your ideas. Finding people who are sympathetic to your point of view usually isn't hard. But make sure that you aren't just talking to people who think the way you do. That's one of the worst, and easiest, mistakes to make. It's very hard to avoid preaching to the converted. If you do, you'll waste your time.

This is one of those recommendations that may sound wrongheaded, but we think it's the key to success. Harvey Robins, an alumnus of the Dinkins administration in New York and one of the city's most influential political commentators, has said that his most valuable connections are the dozen smart people who will always tell him what he's doing wrong. He relies on them to kick his butt a little bit and give him serious critical feedback. These are the people he talks to all the time—but they are hard to find.

For any kind of collaborator, be careful about working with individuals and groups that are rigidly ideological and incapable of compromise. They can limit your flexibility, and they inevitably feel betrayed by any recommendations you make outside of a strict party line.

Let's be clear. When we talk about finding collaborators, we don't mean coalition-building or community organizing. We don't encourage you to create monthly group meetings, agendas, committees, or get people to put lots of time or organizational support behind your idea. You're not creating a new infrastructure. You're building unique relationships with other individuals and organizations, based on mutual respect, to think through what you want accomplished and help you get it done.

At first, these collaborators will mostly have no formal obligation to you or you to them. Some of them are merely people you'll call from time to time when you're working on a new project or want some helpful feedback. But some of them will turn out to be more important partners in the long run.

One final thought on the subject: Collaborating doesn't mean you have to let others make decisions for you, or that you have to adopt their agenda. But you also can't expect others to work with you if you don't let them have any say in what you are selling. You need balance and some practice. Don't be surprised if you have to negotiate some misunderstandings and miscommunications along the way.

A PROJECT PLAN

Now that you know where you're going, it's time to create a roadmap to help you get there. Regardless of your usual work habits, when it comes to a project of this scale, organization and planning are critical. After all, you're trying to structure information so that it's easily understood. A project plan will keep you focused, organize your time and allow you to shift gears partway through if it becomes clear that something isn't working.

Below is a general outline of what needs to be done. As we work our way through the next few chapters, we'll describe in greater detail just how to accomplish these tasks. But before we get into the specifics, you should have an idea of what it will take to create a stunning report and get it noticed.

1. **Research**
   - Preliminary hypothesis and list of sources
   - General investigation
   - Analyze and assess the information
   - Further investigation on specifics
2. **Writing**
   - Focus ideas and recommendations
   - Develop rough structure
   - Choose style and tone
   - Create a first draft
3. **Editing**
   - Input on general direction, structure, examples, focus
   - Write second draft with edit in mind
   - Have outside reviewers give feedback
   - Assess new draft for clarity, accuracy and sharpness of language
   - Write display copy (headlines, pull quotes, etc.)
   - Factcheck
4. **Design**
   - Talk with designer about basics
   - First design
   - Hone design elements
   - Production edits
   - Proofread
   - Print

5. **Distribution**
    - Create a plan, considering political and media context
    - Prepare your supporters
    - Release the report to the press
    - Send the report to others you think should read it
    - Work with allies to spread the findings and recommendations

It sure seems like a lot when you read it all at once. But don't panic—or worse, give up. Each stage is imminently manageable. Some will just take an afternoon. The good news is, many of these steps pay all sorts of dividends beyond the report, from building new alliances to learning how to write more effectively (your grant proposals will be much better after you've written a report or two). And most of the work is fun, interesting or both.

You also might want to consider adding a timetable to your project, to keep it from going on forever. It doesn't have to be too specific, just give a number of weeks for each stage. There's a very good chance that you'll break that schedule, at least a little, but you'll have a yardstick to know if things are dragging. And if you really want to have a report out before, say, the spring legislative session, having a timetable that gives you an idea of some deadline you can't miss is crucial.

But don't worry too much about specifics for either the timetable or the basic workplan. You're looking to plan your time and to keep an eye on what you're trying to accomplish in each stage. The exact details of what will happen down the road are unknowable now anyway; it will depend on your findings.

PUTTING TOGETHER YOUR TEAM

The question is, who's going to do all this work? We assume that you'll probably be relying on other people to do at least some of it. In fact, when it comes to writing and editing, we strongly recommend that at least two people are involved to create a stronger and better written document.

Looking at your organization's staff and their abilities and available time, you can have as few as two or as many as a dozen people involved with your report (remember that managing a large crew can be a job in and of itself). To stay lean and keep on a tight budget, at the Center for an Urban Future, we work with a small staff and hire experienced researchers and writers as projects come up. We've found that paying people to research and write is almost always more efficient than relying on donated efforts. It takes stamina and concentration to get through this process. Volunteers, however well-intentioned, often have to deal with too many competing pressures.

In hiring freelance writers and editors, we usually look for a blend of the following:

- A strong interest in public policy issues
- Quality writing experience and published articles ("clips," in journalist jargon)
- Flexibility and a willingness to listen to new ideas
- A reporter's instinct for tracking down good sources
- Excitement and enthusiasm for the work

It may seem strange to say, but ignorance can be your ally. You don't need to hire a policy guru to make your project a success. In fact, *hiring an expert in your subject can be a mistake.*

RESOURCES

Journalists To Go

Do you like the idea of working with a journalist but are at a loss for finding one for hire? Fear not, the Internet has an answer for *that* problem too. Try visiting these websites:

- Mediabistro.com
- Journalismjobs.com
- Monster.com
- Guru.com

The job listings here are frequented by really good journalists (who are often excited to work on a project that is for a good cause).

Their preconceived notions and agendas can actually interfere with the process, since they may not listen to ideas that contradict what they already "know." More commonly, they may not be able to get away from insider jargon and may be so wrapped up in the issue that they can't explain the big picture to an outsider.

The best person to hire is someone with tremendous curiosity, a real enthusiasm for the subject, good reporting and writing skills, and an open mind. That person will be most successful at getting to the heart of the issue and best able to explain it to other intelligent laymen.

WHO'S THE BOSS?

Managing your team well is important, even if it's only a team of one. If you're not doing the research yourself, at the bare minimum, check in once in a while to make sure the process isn't off on some tangent, to brainstorm new sources of information and to hone in on the most promising angles and ideas. Talk things through again when the writing is about to start to help set the tone and overall perspective and to make sure your writer can write. During the writing and editing, we suggest you check in more frequently so the report doesn't go astray or lose its focus.

Community groups are often run collectively or with a loosely defined hierarchy where decisions are made collaboratively. Here, that's not going to work. You'll need to pick an authority and give that person ultimate control of the writing process. You don't need to create a tyrant—the person in charge must be willing to listen to other people's concerns and critiques. *But writing and editing by committee is always fatal.*

Usually, the person with that ultimate control is not the writer but the editor. He or she sets the deadlines, exercises judgment and decides when the document is ready to move on to the next stage. In disagreements between the writer and the editor, the editor has final say.

You'd think that we always take the role of editor on our projects, but at the Center that is rarely the case. We actually hire freelancers to edit most of our projects (including this one), preferring to do the networking and hard research ourselves. But after we turn over the first draft, the editor runs the show. We know what we want to say; they help us tell our story clearly, concisely and with punch.

CHAPTER FOUR

Doing the Research

Doing the Research

Your infrastructure is finally in place. You know what you're going to report on, and who's in charge of what. You've considered who are your allies and what kind of response your findings might create. You are ready for the heart and soul of creating your report: gathering information.

By the time you're done with this stage, you will have a deep and broad understanding of your topic, a long list of who is affected by and who can change the current situation, and an exciting collection of ideas for fixing those problems.

Whatever you think about the subject, be genuinely committed to collecting opinions from the widest possible range of sources. While your own perspective will no doubt be foremost, in order to be credible and develop a truly defensible position, you must be thorough and thoughtful—and that means keeping your mind open.

In 1999, the City University of New York (CUNY) was in the headlines because Mayor Giuliani was trying to stop the system from offering remediation classes. Liberals around the city were outraged by what seemed like the end of an opportunity for low-income students, and we decided to do a report on what exactly remediation provided. However, call-

When you're done with this stage, you will have a deep understanding of your topic, a long list of who can change the current situation and ideas for fixing the problems.

ing around to academics and other experts around the country, we quickly discovered that while offering remediation wasn't much of an indicator about how well community colleges served low-income constituents, how the colleges were integrated into economic development programs was.

In New York, though, nobody was even asking about CUNY and economic development—everyone was too busy lobbing bombs back and forth about remediation. We decided to change the entire focus of our report, and when the final product was released, we grabbed the attention of the head of CUNY, the mayor's economic development people and more than a few journalists. If we had limited our reporting to the usual suspects on "our" side of the remediation debate—and if we hadn't asked some broad questions that went beyond our assumptions about how remediation works—we would have just been one more voice in a political fight that, in the end, really went nowhere.

This section is tailored toward writing a big report with unimpeachable research, noteworthy findings and workable recommendations. (In Chapter Six, we'll give some brief tips on other documents that you may want to produce later on: press releases, postcard campaigns, public service announcements, briefing papers, news alerts and so forth.) Even if you're not quite ready for a really big report, we suggest you read through this chapter and the next, which covers writing and editing. Much of the process we describe can be applied to any writing project.

HISTORY LESSON

Before you make a single phone call, talk through a preliminary hypothesis. What's your focus? What do you think your research will tell you? For example, if you're looking into allegations of police misconduct toward minorities, you might assume problems arise because the force is largely white and poorly trained in cultural sensitivity. These hypotheses may well change as you learn more, but having a clear starting point will help. Sometimes our most basic assumptions about an issue are proven wrong. More often, you'll modify or fine-tune them on the basis of what you learn. But by recognizing how you view the topic, you can make sure your blind spots don't cause you to ignore any sources or points of view.

Maybe your perspective on an issue is completely fresh and new and has never been considered before. That's unlikely. But even if it's true, *your issue still has a history. Learn it.* You'll need to be aware of and incorporate past perspectives and viewpoints into your own position. If you are successful at putting together a powerful policy agenda, people will ask you for your opinions concerning this subject (that's why you're doing this, right?). *City Limits*, for example, is recognized for its expertise on housing policy in New York City.

Other reporters sometimes call wanting to know which mayors have put the most money into public housing or which 1970s slumlord was the city's worst. It really helps to have at least a general grasp of this kind of information. If you don't know what's already been said, you'll lose traction in the public policy debate. Imagine being on a local TV talk show, unaware that your suggestion for changing the local recycling rules was found wanting ten years ago by a university study. How are you going to look trying to answer that question?

You're also likely to find out some interesting things in the process. As we've said before, many policy writers can't or won't make their findings accessible to ordinary readers. But that doesn't mean that their thinking wasn't valuable. Assess their conclusions for yourself. You may find that you just need to re-package some of what they said—of course, giving them credit for it.

LOOKING FOR DATA

Throughout your interviews and library research, keep an eye out for facts and figures that you can adapt in your report. Your aim is to build a persuasive argument, and to do that, you're going to need more than opinions (even if you have a lot of different people's opinions). Anticipate that *many people will try to dismiss your report as biased or one-sided.* Other groups' data can be a very convincing part of a policy argument, and including their findings also shows that others are concerned about the same topics.

Data might come from formal academic or government research. It could be information collected from a study of a neighborhood by a community group or from a survey conducted by a union or business trade association. As long as the data is public and you credit the source, you can use it in your work. (You can also do your own research. We cover that in "Survey Says" on page 60.)

For any data from an outside source, do at least a cursory sniff test. Make sure that the numbers you're borrowing make sense, and aren't slanted or shoddily done. And be sure you see the results yourself; don't depend on someone saying offhand, "The mayor cut funding by 30 percent." Find the budgets and compare them, or at least find a group you trust that published an analysis of the budgets.

"The two greatest barriers for a group to overcome are a) the lack of time of most decision makers, and b) the impression

Five Reporters' Rules to Borrow:

1) Go there in person whenever possible.
2) Ask every person you interview for the names of five others you should talk to.
3) Policy is always about people as much as ideas. Who stands to benefit? Who will suffer?
4) Always ask: How do you know that? What is your source of information? Where did you get that figure?
5) Scrupulously honor any promises of confidentiality.

that research is biased and exaggerated," says MassINC's Neil Mello. "In general, decision-makers are skeptical of most policy research and see a slant. They also know the vast majority of problems are not at a crisis level and that research tends to exaggerate. So we work hard at attaining credibility. We focus on being independent and truthful."

Most people will be grateful if you give their work more exposure. Whether you use a table of data from a study, quote them in your report or ask them to stand up and take questions with you at a press conference, it's pretty rare to find someone who doesn't want their work used. It's also a good way to make new friends. Of course, this is only true if you aren't distorting it or taking it far out of context, which we don't recommend in any case. Once you get tarred with that brush, it's hard to rebuild your credibility.

JOURNALISM'S JOB

When we talk about acting like a reporter, we don't mean one of the numbskulls that hang around on the lawns of celebrities. We're referring to serious investigative journalism, the kind that uncovers real stories, shows how ordinary people cope with day-to-day problems and holds politicians accountable for the things they do with our money (Think "60 Minutes" or "Nightline").

We strive to emulate the actions of a good reporter:

- Develop an informed analysis of the issue.
- Understand the political dimensions of the topic.
- Find powerful anecdotes to illustrate our points.
- Never forget the human side of any policy issue.
- Always keep in mind who may benefit or lose from a

particular decision.
- Know the history of the debate.
- Be able to explain the arguments on all sides.

Approaching this project as a journalist means understanding that people themselves are your best sources of ideas and information–not the written word. *One face-to-face conversation is worth five phone interviews* because establishing rapport is much easier. Don't even think about interviewing someone by email. You can go to a book or a report for background information (and we give you some tips on how to do that effectively starting on page 55) but you can only get the enlightening, informative dialogue we are looking for—the conversations that really spark good ideas—from another person. It's also the best way to get the latest information and hear about your community's specific issues and problems.

THE ART OF THE INTERVIEW

In interviews, your goal is to get the most informed and interesting people to talk openly and honestly with you. How do you do it? For one thing, you've got to leave your opinions behind. You can't come thinking you'll convince your interview subject that you are right and that he or she is wrong. At this point, *your goal is not to change anyone's mind but your own.* Focus on listening well and communicating your seriousness and willingness to listen.

Not everyone is articulate, but even people who aren't often have something interesting to say. Be patient and ask clear, defined questions–it will help get you the information you want. Make sure to take notes. Whether you do it copiously or sparingly is up to you and how good your memory is. Some people use tape recorders. Usually, it's easier to just scribble it down on the spot. Regardless, keep an ear open for good quotes—anything especially powerful, interesting, witty or that just sums things up well. Including direct quotes in your final report from experts on a topic shows that you spoke with thoughtful, well-versed people, and didn't just come to your conclusions on your own.

RESOURCES

To Find Out More...

These sites have some smart tips on interviewing someone for an investigative story. They might come across as a little hard-boiled for your purposes, but the underlying points are good advice.

- http://home.earthlink.net/~cassidyny/naldertip.htm
- http://home.earthlink.net/~cassidyny/practicaladvice.htm

Be clear ahead of time whether or not your source is willing to be quoted, and about how she/he should be identified. For some people, it would jeopardize their jobs or their status in the community if others know they talked so frankly with you, so accommodate their need for confidentiality and honor it, especially since you want real candor. Sometimes an interview subject will agree later to be quoted on one specific point.

People may ask, before consenting to an interview, if they'll be able to read through your draft before it goes to press. If you don't want to show your entire report to someone who may argue about sections that he or she doesn't even appear in, ask if you can instead just run their information by them at the end, for factchecking. Often, people ask to read the draft just to be sure they aren't misquoted or have their name spelled wrong. How you handle people asking to see some or all of your draft

HOT TIP

What Do I Ask?

A few good starting questions:

- If you could change one thing about this situation, what would it be? Who or what stands in the way?
- What mistakes keep getting made with this issue? Why?
- Which politicians or other powerful people are interested in this issue, why, and what stand do they take?
- What's been getting better? What's worse?

is up to you, but we strongly recommend that you be consistent. It's only fair, and it protects you from charges of bias. If you're going to let one person do it, you should be willing to let anyone else who asks do it too.

WHO'S WHO

Finding smart people to talk about your issue isn't difficult because, frankly, *most people like to tell you what they think.* Ask around for tips—ask everyone you think might have suggestions. Cast the broadest net you can, and write down every contact, even if you don't think you'll use it. You never know when you might find that the person's perspective is exactly what you needed.

This stage is serious hard work. Expect to start with at least 100 phone calls. Out of those 100 contacts, you'll probably be able to reach 80, and of those 80 you'll probably get 40 to 50 useful conversations. Ultimately, only a handful may be truly essential to your report. But if you don't start huge, you'll never find that handful of crucial contacts. And the ones who don't make it into your report are valuable as contacts in your database and potential allies once your report is released. Besides, there's no better way to become known as a key thinker on an issue than to sit down and listen to people who care about it.

This may sound like overkill, but it is key to doing great work. You want to be convinced, by the end of your reporting, that there isn't a single person left to talk to that might have something important to say.

Good people to talk to include:

Member organizations
Representatives from unions, community groups, political clubs, other organized groups. Some of these organizations do their own valuable research; some simply have a strong stake in your issues.

Policymakers and politicians
You should reach out to both elected and appointed officials.

More importantly, get to know their staff members, who often have a powerful, if less visible, influence over policy. Find out what they think and ask them what laws and rules they've developed and supported. Ask questions now, and you'll be better prepared to lobby them later.

Government employees

Beyond the muckety-mucks who make the rules, make sure to reach out to the people who actually have to put the rules into practice—caseworkers, inspectors, bureau managers, etc. These people are closer to the problem, and may understand the situation better than anyone else. Unfortunately, they often lack the clout to do anything about it, or may be afraid to stick their necks out. You, on the other hand, can adopt their good ideas. These people also know exactly which documents, records and rules are kept on file about your issue. Some people in government may not be willing to talk with you, for fear of retribution or out of mistrust, but it's always worth a try.

Private sector leaders, consultants and opinionmakers

They sit on the boards of nonprofits; they are asked to testify at City Council hearings and to serve on task forces appointed by the Governor. Sometimes they are motivated by personal experience; sometimes by the hope of a contract or a job; sometimes by a desire to contribute to the community's well-being. They are worth consulting for their influence and expertise.

People directly affected by the problem or policy

Listen to their stories. They will teach you about the issue and eventually help you make your points. Unfortunately, *policy problems are often confusing and boring. Real-life stories will dramatize the issue* and make it compelling to your audience.

Talk directly to people affected by the policies you want to change. Also talk to people working closely with them. Keep your eyes peeled for somebody articulate and persuasive whose life is changed by the issue. Ask them now if they might be interested in talking to the press later on, should that come up. (It'll really help you to have a few contacts like that when you are getting reporters interested in your story.) Make sure to ask people's permission before you use their names and stories in your writing. If you must, change their names and identifying characteristics—but try to avoid it. You lose credibility that way.

SEE FOR YOURSELF

We can't emphasize enough the importance of that last group: You're not done interviewing until you've spoken with some people affected by the policy you're studying. This is what will separate you from everybody else. You want people to have a powerful, palpable sense of your knowledge of the issue, and the only way you'll get that kind of expertise is first hand. You're going to want your readers to be able to feel the grime in the unemployment office when you talk about welfare, to see the kids sharing notebooks when you write about school overcrowding.

Doing your own fact-finding—seeing things with your own eyes and hearing with your own ears—is crucial. These are probably the most important ideas we take from journalism: the idea that reporting is always better than relying on common knowledge; seeing it yourself is always better than hearing about it; and there is no substitute for first-hand information. Always go visit a place in person, if you can. If your sources can spare the time, arrange to meet them face-to-face.

Many people may not bother with it, but it's essential. *Conducting original research gives you credibility.* You aren't just spewing out received wisdom, or copying the ideas and opinions of the people who came before you. You're generating your own independent analysis.

When you go to original sources—the people affected by public policy and those who make the policies—you also open up your mind to new ideas. By deliberately exposing yourself to a variety of perspectives and experiences, you'll be more confident in the end that your stance is right. It'll give your conclusions a weight and power that you can't get any other way. And you'll collect completely new data to bolster your argument.

When the Center for an Urban Future wanted to find out what businesses that provide stable, well-paying jobs to low-skilled New Yorkers needed to thrive, we thought of the two city airports, which are huge employers that had been neglected by government and policy experts. So our research director Jonathan Bowles became an airport regular. He spent weeks hanging out there, talking with everybody he could think of.

"I tried to find the experts—company chiefs, airport boosters and insiders, leaders who really speak for the industry. Everywhere I went, I would try to get five or 10 recommendations for other interviews. I tried to arrange tours whenever possible, of the airports and the areas around the airports. I'd write down the names of all the companies, and I'd call them.

I would walk around the cargo areas of the airports, knocking on doors. I would introduce myself and explain that I was working on a report about airport issues and ask people my questions. I found some good sources that way.

"Going door to door, you can also get corroboration and make sure you have the story straight. I often say things like, 'I have heard that this is a big problem—can you tell me if it's true?' That way, you get that backup and sometimes you get a good anecdote as well."

Bowles' legwork paid off in other ways, as well. Some of the local cargo operators suggested he talk with companies that had moved to nearby Nassau County. When he arrived, he discovered a thriving enclave of airport service firms that had been crowded out of the city. Jobs and tax revenues lost to the suburbs became one of the themes of the final report.

After the report was released, Bowles had several meetings with cargo officials and government representatives, including the local congressman. "Talking to companies and at airports gave me credibility and trust that really helped those meetings go well," he says. A month later, *Crain's New York Business* reported that the NY/NJ Port Authority started a study of cargo access at Kennedy, an issue that simply wasn't being considered before our report. A lot of work went into the final product, but Bowles credits his time at and around the airport for much of the success. "You can't talk to ten people and then write a report," he says.

IS THAT TRUE?

Here comes that old canard: Just because you saw it in the

HOT TIP

A Rule Of Journalism That Many Reporters Ignore But You Shouldn't

Confirm any controversial allegations from at least two independent, unrelated sources.

newspaper (or on the web) doesn't mean it's true. And the same goes for people, who don't always represent themselves accurately or give correct information.

There are different ways to figure out whether or not your sources are good. With people, institutional affiliation definitely makes it more likely that someone isn't a crackpot, just as information published in a respected daily newspaper or monthly magazine is more likely to be reliable than a hand-printed brochure. More likely, but it's no guarantee. Ideologues, cranks and liars can get tenure or a newspaper column, too. *Be skeptical of everyone, no matter how grand their title or how nice their suit.* Be democratic in your skepticism: Don't automatically assume that the powerful are lying or that the poor are telling the truth (or vice versa).

Most often, people don't really lie. Instead, they tell you with all confidence and self-assurance that something is fact, and much later, you'll find out that it was a garbled version of a third-hand rumor. Substantiate people's assertions without offending them. You can say, "I'd like to know more about that.

Where did you get that information? Who has studied this in a systematic way?" We're certainly not telling you only to trust information from established sources. It's only that you have to develop your own nose and your own techniques for validating information, and apply them scrupulously.

WRITTEN SOURCES

Of course, not everything you need can be gleaned from interviews. One general piece of advice: Go to the web before you trek over to the library. The Internet has many new sources of information for researchers, and many of the old sources, like libraries and newspaper archives, are available online in searchable indexes and catalogs. You'll find public policy groups you had no idea existed, dissertations on your subject, campaigns in other states focused on your issue, and probably a few obsessed oddballs too. You may also find interesting listservs—email-based discussion groups.

On the web and off, these are some of the categories of information to keep your eyes open for:

Reports, research and articles on the topic

Keep a very open mind about where these can come from, including popular press, trade journals, independent policy organizations, think tanks, umbrella associations, government agencies and unions.

Public policy polls

Looking at old data can give you a history of public opinion on your issue, and new polls might bolster your argument about where policies should change.

Academic sources

Not every topic will have been the subject of an academic paper, but when it has, you can often find data and opinions that are well-documented and relatively unbiased. Look at journals, books and conference proceedings.

Government records

When you are writing about areas of public policy, government documents can be a real treasure. How bad is school overcrowding in your neighborhood? How many contracts

INFORMATION

FOIA Your Information

The federal Freedom of Information Act and the state equivalents can unlock a wealth of solid information, but you've got to know what you're looking for and ask for it the right way. You also have to be patient.

Start by asking informally for the government records you seek. Be as specific as possible without limiting yourself. Ask, for example, for "all records relating to the expense of removing alligators from Central Park, including contracts, line items and personnel records." You can start with the telephone, or write a letter. Keep records of when and who you asked.

If you get no response, and you really want the data, consider a FOIA. Make sure you are asking the right agency, and make sure you're asking for the right paperwork first. (A friend who works in government or a sympathetic bureaucrat may be able to help you figure out which kinds of documents to ask for.) For more specific information on filing a successful FOIA, go to the Reporters Committee for Freedom of the Press (rcfp.org) or the National Freedom of Information Coalition (nfoic.org). If you follow their samples closely, and are persistent and polite in your follow-up, you stand a fair chance of getting what you're looking for. Patience is the key.

were given out last year for health services? Government agencies track this kind of information. Remember that your city, county and state likely keep their own sets of records in addition to the federal government's data. Some information you can get just by asking; sometimes, you'll have to file a Freedom of Information Act request.

SURVEY SAYS

To make your work more credible—and to add a "news hook" to your report—you may want to adopt some techniques of formal or academic research in your own work. These techniques can:

- Test out your assumptions with a more organized, less arbitrary approach
- Provide input and perspective from a wider group of individuals or organizations
- Make your findings and recommendations more credible in the eyes of others

The Idaho Community Action Network, organizers who work on issues affecting low-income communities, conducted a "consumer testing project" that asked 25 families that clearly qualified for government-sponsored health insurance to apply to the program. Since the group wasn't a random sample, the network couldn't know for certain that the experiences were typical. But they could get a general idea of how long the process took and how effective it was. The results pointed to a need for a simpler application form and a toll-free information hotline, recommendations in their final report that were soon instituted.

Sometimes, the sample of "subjects" you need to conduct a poll or survey is right at your fingertips. If your organization does social service work, you can write about your own programs as a way of making a point about larger social policies—explaining why, for example, certain rules and regulations put additional pressure on your clients. You could ask your clients if they want to participate in a study and tell them you will use that information to argue for changes that will benefit them and others like them.

That said, be careful not to exploit people who are relying on you for help. Make sure your study safeguards their right to privacy and their right to be left alone. If you have an institutional review board, you must talk to them, too.

Experts will judge your findings by examining how you collected your information and arrived at your conclusions. For example, try to be diverse when building a representative group of people, companies or organizations to survey. Map out the universe of the people who are concerned about your topic, and then document that you have talked to representatives from all sides (e.g. "After interviewing landlords, tenants, housing inspectors, real estate brokers, tenant organizers, contractors, mortgage lenders and building managers, we determined that...").

If your questions are more focused—like the Idaho Community Action Network's interest in families eligible for health insurance—you can still be diverse. Make sure you don't only talk with people on the south side of town, for instance, or those who also receive food stamps and welfare. Repeating your questions with a large group of sources also

HOT TIP

Where to Find It

If you're not experienced with searching the web for your topic, figuring out where to start can be a bit intimidating. Here's some tips.

Our favorite Internet search engine

- Google (google.com) includes searches of PDF files: the document format that many academics and policy people use on the web. Also, check out their government-only search engine.

Top electronic databases

These are expensive to rent, but your library may offer free access.

- Lexis-Nexis has comprehensive newspaper, magazine and legal records (lexis-nexis.com).
- ProQuest is a trove of academic, trade, popular magazine and major newspaper articles (proquest.com).

Policy sites

Here are a few national organizations that may have written about your issue. Also check their lists of links to other good sources.

- The Center for Budget and Policy Priorities (cbpp.org)
- The Urban Institute (urbaninstitute.org)
- The Heritage Foundation (heritage.org)
- The Electronic Policy Network (epn.org)
- Handsnet (handsnet.org)
- Newspaper Links (newspaperlinks.com)

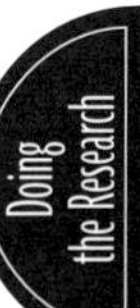

makes your conclusions more reliable. It's great to be able to write something like: "Our informal survey of 30 local teachers revealed that..."

Finally, make sure that you have a checklist of questions that you ask every source. It might be three questions to ask over the telephone, a more detailed questionnaire to administer during a site visit, or discussion points for a focus group. The important thing for a survey is consistency.

ANALYZING YOUR RESEARCH

The time will come to stop interviewing and start analyzing. Maybe you've been hearing the same answers over and over, and you've pretty well covered the range of opinions. Or maybe you feel like you need to think through what you've already gathered, in order to start asking more specific and focused questions. If you're doing a survey, maybe you've reached as many people as you can.

Before you move on, look back at your initial hypothesis about what needs to be done. If all your reading and interviews hasn't challenged your original ideas (and even possibly changed some of them), you probably haven't talked to the right people.

To get your ideas in some kind of order—and be warned: that can be much harder than it sounds, considering all the sources and opinions you've uncovered—try to boil things down into a few overarching points. Any report should be able to be described in one or two sentences—that's your guiding star as you write and edit. Everything should point to that star: your examples, your reasons for the problem, your recommendations, etc. And as you think about what those few sentences say, keep in mind two very important criteria: 1) what are you trying to convey beyond the obvious points, and 2) what is the news value.

For example, in our CUNY report, we had a few underlying themes. One was that, despite what the mayor was saying about how the system wasn't doing a good job, CUNY did have some notable successes—including very important companies that were paying CUNY programs to train their workers. Another point was that schools around the city had successful economic development projects, giving local reporters a hook no matter what community they covered. And finally, we knew we could make recommendations well within the scope of what was politically and financially possible. With those basic ideas in mind, it was a lot easier to decide what arguments and examples we should emphasize and what just couldn't fit. (And some interesting ideas just don't fit in almost any report.)

BACK AND FORTH

If it seems like we're starting to slide into advice on writing the report a little early, you're right. But that's not a surprise, because this part of the process tends to blur the distinction between research and writing. You may take a crack at typing up a few pages of executive summary overview to help your thoughts gel near the end of research, or you might need to stop halfway through writing the first draft to call back several sources to help you think through a particularly knotty issue.

One bit of research that will likely continue until near the very end is a search for anecdotes, quotes or data to back up your assertions. As you really sharpen your thesis on the page, you'll realize exactly what will "prove" what you're trying to say. *Don't be afraid to call someone back a second (or third or fourth) time to get more information from them*—either to search for a new example or to give some specifics about something you've already heard. That's another lesson from journalism: As you learn more, you find out what else you need to ask.

CHAPTER FIVE

Creating the Report

Creating the Report

Organizing, writing, editing and design will determine the fate of your work: whether or not people will read it, how much of it they'll read, and whether or not any of it sticks in their heads. You're fighting tune-out: that very natural tendency of people to put down whatever it is they are reading and take a nap or make a grilled-cheese sandwich instead. *Your main enemy is overkill.* Think of the pile of letters, reports, magazines and newsletters on your desk and the list of unread emails on your computer. Your goal is to get people to take the time to read and remember your astute observations and clever recommendations for change.

That doesn't mean all is lost if you are not a naturally skilled writer. We won't go through every writing exercise around (consider one of many great writing textbooks for that kind of help), but we will go through some tips on getting your best ideas on the page for this kind of report. One of the best ways to ensure your report is clear and interesting is to have an editor work it over, and we'll talk about that too. Finally, making your report look handsome and clear on the page will also bolster your message.

Step One: The First Draft

Even professional writers can loathe starting a new project. The most daunting stage of the entire process is usually sitting down in front of the computer with dozens of ideas in your head, notes from scores on interviews on your desk and a blank computer screen in front of you. Take a deep breath. By following some basic principles, getting a first draft can be relatively pain-free.

> We suggest writing the first draft without worrying about how you put things. And even during the first edit, your main concern is to hone your ideas to really work.

Throughout the writing and editing process, you're likely to stumble at times on the simple fact that you can't get ideas onto paper without using words. Sometimes the ideas are good, but the words aren't quite right—and sometimes the words read very well, but that hides the fact that the ideas aren't really what you want to say. We suggest writing the first draft without worrying too much about how you put things. (Within reason, of course. You want to make sense.) And even during the first edit, your main concern is to hone those ideas so they really work. When it comes to a choice between "if" or "whether" and how the punctuation works, there's time for that at the end.

YOUR RECOMMENDATIONS

Usually there are two elements to a policy paper: the argument that sums up your take on the current situation and the recommendations for change. Which one you write first is your decision, but we think it's easier to write the recommendations first. It helps structure your writing and keep you focused.

Ideally, at this point you'll have some solid conclusions about what needs to be done, and those will naturally lend themselves to recommendations. But keep other considerations in mind, especially the political climate. You should think about what's possible as well as what's the right thing to do. When writing recommendations, think: Whose mind do you need to change?

To assemble our recommendations, we try to use these guidelines:

Identify the solutions that make sense to everybody

Find areas of consensus among the different stakeholders you interviewed, and turn those into specific proposals. Those ideas will garner wide support.

Think carefully about asking for public funds

When asking for more money to be spent on the problem, be able to justify the amount you call for. There aren't a lot of public funds available these days, so try to keep your financial wish list short.

Spread responsibility around

Ask corporations to make private investments or submit to environmental regulation, ask state contractors to agree to new efficiency standards, or suggest that community members participate in a planning process.

Be clear and catchy

Dress up simple ideas and old-but-good proposals in sharp, eye-catching language. Often the most successful recommendations aren't the most radical. They are just the simplest or the clearest.

Be savvy

Figure out how to make your research dovetail with current policy concerns, and take account of what ideas hold sway.

Be provocative

Bring a fresh perspective to tired policy debates with new ideas, smart language and a sharp perspective.

It's worth going into detail about asking for public funds. You may very well feel that to solve the problems you've identified, the government will need to increase some budgets. If that's the case, it's critical to be clear about why the money is needed.

For example, in order to call attention to how children's mental health services were underfunded, the Citizens' Committee for Children decided to come up with a number that spoke for itself. By calculating how many children in New York State were estimated to have serious mental problems, the cost of insurance and the average cost of treatment, they came up with a bill for $356 million—almost twice as much money as state government was spending. The authors knew that politically it was quite impossible to raise funding to that level, but it illustrated the point very well: The demand was enormous, and the supply inadequate. By putting the problem into context, the campaign was able to push the state to add another $40 million to the budget—a 20 percent increase and the single largest new allocation of funds for children's mental health services in state history.

ORGANIZATION

You can use the traditional structure of many policy reports, with a set introduction, methodology, findings, conclusions and so on. We don't usually use this system, because it can be boring. Instead, we try to tell a story that supports our conclusions and recommendations. For our piece on how September 11th affected New York's arts community, for example, we started with one sentence; "Artists may live for applause, but they can't live on it." We immediately followed through with what we call a "one-two punch." First, tell the readers what we're saying: "The arts sector has witnessed severe blows to all three of its core funding streams—earned income from ticket sales and other sources, contributed income from wealthy individuals and foundations, and government funding...[And] most arts organizations simply have no safety net."

And then we explained why they should care: "Arts organizations are responsible for 130,000 jobs and contribute $13 billion to the local economy." From there, we went through the research and facts that supported those arguments. Hopefully, we had captured the readers' attention so they continued on into the report to read the details.

Whichever structure you choose, know what you want to say. It's tedious, but write an outline first. You don't have to rigidly adhere to it, but an outline is invaluable for keeping focused. And refer back to your outline frequently to keep on track.

Decide about how long the report should be in advance, based on the scope and importance of your topic and the amount of research you conducted. Keep in mind that *longer is always worse.* The faster you can say something, the more likely it is that someone will read it.

Divide the document into a few sections. One option is to create segments that highlight different elements of the topic. In one issue of *Child Welfare Watch*, our biannual report that investigates one aspect of NYC's foster care system, we split a complicated discussion of family court into separate sections covering topics like the information presented to judges, the pay scale for court-appointed lawyers, the number of cases flooding the system, and the fate of an ambitious reform. Except for a brief overview in the introduction,

HOT TIP

Author, Author

Don't forget to include a spot for a description of your organization and contact information, so people know who produced this masterpiece. And if any individuals or groups are affiliated with this project or your organization, they'll want to be noted as well. We usually have a box on the last page for this information.

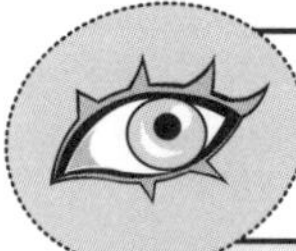

CASE STUDY

Visualize This

More Ed, More Bread

Higher education correlates with higher income, and has become worth more over time.

♂	High School Dropout	High School Diploma	Some College or Associate's Degree	Bachelor's Degree	Graduate Degree
1959	$22,648	$30,348	$36,202	$45,310	$44,258
1979	$28,517	$37,778	$41,714	$51,704	$55,427
1998	$21,927	$31,859	$38,910	$56,332	$71,971
♀					
1959	$9,644	$13,053	$14,986	$18,568	$24,208
1979	$12,531	$16,422	$18,685	$22,070	$30,366
1998	$12,952	$19,217	$24,331	$32,721	$43,941

Source: College Board Review, May 2001

For our report "Building a Highway to Higher Ed," we included this chart almost as an afterthought. It had some interesting information, but these statistics weren't the main point we were trying to establish. Since publication, the numbers have been about the most quoted part of our entire report. Just goes to show the power of presenting information clearly.

no section tried to explain the whole picture. But taken together, the report gave a clear picture of a complicated problem.

We don't usually break things up quite so much, but we always try to structure a report to make digesting its information as easy as possible. Regardless of your structure, your reader will appreciate it if you follow these rules:

- Have an introduction and/or executive summary for those who won't read any further.
- If you want to introduce your recommendations one by one in the course of the main text, make sure that they are repeated in their own separate section as well. Some people will want to skip right to a summary list.
- Footnotes probably aren't necessary, but you could include a list of sources or a bibliography at the end of the report.
- If you conducted formal research, one short section can describe your process and methodology.

Make sure to give your readers something to look at. Supporting charts or tables that make data visual. Sidebars with anecdotes or case studies. Boxes of text with short, well-edited excerpts from interviews. Brief descriptions of how other cities and states have dealt with the same problem. All convey information in a slightly different way, and make your points easier to absorb. Nothing is more daunting to a reader of a policy report than opening up to a page of pure, undifferentiated text.

CHOOSE YOUR CONTEXT

Put your message in context. Otherwise, someone else will do it for you, and you may not like it. ("Tax-and-spend liberal" and "divisive partisan" are two perennials.) As you're writing, keep in mind the theme that underlays your message, whether or not you make it explicit. What kinds of ideas strike a chord with people? Here are a few classics:

- Fairness
- Freedom
- Equal opportunity
- Sharing prosperity
- Giving all children a chance
- Supporting families
- Common sense
- Spending taxpayers' money wisely
- Self-reliance and independence

Who is going to say publicly that they don't care about fairness or about giving children a future? Later, when you go out and create a buzz around your finished report, you can tightly target your message. For now, just make sure that you're sensitive to how your message is framed in the larger debate.

WHAT'S YOUR STORY?

One of the unwritten rules of journalism is that a story must have three things: a conflict, a hook and an angle. Trying for at least two will make your writing more compelling and livelier.

The Conflict

Explain clearly the vested interests people hold on both sides. Who is being harmed by the current policies and how? Who benefits from the situation? What motivates people to take this stand?

INFORMATION

A Word About Policy Words

One great field guide to common pitfalls of policy writing is Tony Proscio's *In Other Words*, a screed against jargon and insider lingo in the foundation world. It's short, funny and right on target: Proscio's larger point is that jargon makes it hard for ordinary people to understand public policy and therefore undermines dialogue and public input.

He also offers a lot of advice on how to avoid this in your own writing. One of our favorite sections suggests setting up your own list of forbidden words: "As you sit through meetings—the boring ones are best for this—start a list of all the buzz-phrases you hear others overusing," he writes. "The fact that these phrases annoy you should be reason enough to avoid them yourself. Yet you may be surprised (and humbled) to discover that you do not, in fact, always avoid them."

He also makes some excellent recommendations for simple, clear policy writing. Best of all, his booklet is free from the Edna McConnell Clark Foundation (212-551-9100).

The Hook

What's the news here? What makes this timely and relevant? Generally, you introduce the hook somewhere in the beginning. Within the first 400 words, you need to explain to people why they should read your research now. Besides a conflict, The Project for Excellence in Journalism has identified a few other typical hooks.

- Historical outlook: How the current news fits into history
- Horse race: Who is winning and who is losing
- Wrongdoing exposed: The uncovering of scandal or injustice

The Angle

This is less obvious than the hook and has to do more with your tone and analysis. Basically, your angle is what you add to the bare facts of the matter: your well-justified point of view, a way of thinking about the issue that doesn't ram your opinion down your readers' throats. It's more like a way to frame the issue at hand.

GETTING DOWN TO BASICS

Writing well is difficult and for most people, takes a lot of practice. Your goal is a lucid, short, well-documented argument. This does not mean you are "dumbing down" all your research and hard work. You are simplifying, clarifying, making the abstract concrete. *Reaching your audience means bringing your agenda down to a few easy-to-get-across points.* The clearer your thinking is, the easier this will be. Keep in mind that you have, at most, five minutes to engage a reader. So how do you write something that will be so fascinating that your reader will be unwilling to put it down?

Use a provocative, informative lead

Throw out the summation of what the report contains—or better yet, use it as the "nut" down a few paragraphs into the introduction. Start instead with an anecdote or idea that grabs the reader's attention.

Make the most of executive summaries, subheads and introductions

Eyes glaze over when confronted with a page of solid text—help your reader out with quick signposts to what ideas are buried in the text.

Put dry policy implications into real-world terms

Explain just who is affected (numbers always help to show the scope of the problem) and consider some case studies from your research that drive home the human costs of how things work.

HOT TIP

On Brevity

Policy reports typically go to 30 or 40 pages. Ours are rarely more than 20. What we cut out is a lot of repetition and unnecessary language. Aim to say things once (maybe twice to get the point across).

Lose the insider jargon.

All areas of public policy have their own acronyms and technical language. But you want people who aren't necessarily experts in the minutiae of your field—like reporters, concerned citizens and lawmakers—to read your report. If you must use these terms, always include an explanation (sometimes we even create our own simple terms to fill in for a complicated description).

Finally, don't assume that your reader shares your point of view. Whether or not they agree with you, ideological language and a stridently political tone turns people off, and all your independent research will come across like rhetoric—or even a snow job. Your points will be taken much more seriously if you use objective language and rely on the power of your arguments and research to make your point.

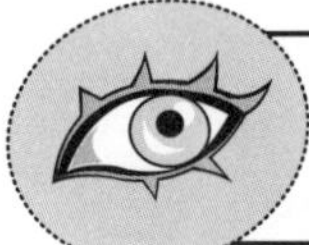

CASE STUDY

Headline News

When you're naming your report, don't scare readers away with a dry title that shouts "boring." Rather, try something more catchy, like these:

➘ **"Ticket to Nowhere"** This report by the Education Trust revealed that huge numbers of high school students who go to college fail or drop out because they were unprepared. Which are you more interested in, the cover pictured below or something entitled "The Importance of College Prep Work at the High-School Level for Students At Risk of Academic Underacheivement During Their Post-Secondary Education"?

Thinking K-16

Vol. 3, Issue 2 A Publication of The Education Trust Fall 1999

TICKET TO NOWHERE

The Gap Between Leaving High School and Entering College and High-Performance Jobs

Dear Reader: Each fall, thousands of high school graduates and their parents are shattered to learn that the high school diploma they collected the previous June is not quite what they thought it would be. Instead of a ticket to college or work, that diploma is, at best, a ticket…back to high school.

Many of these students may, indeed, have been *admitted* to college. But they scored so low on the college's placement examination that they wound up in remedial courses. Others may have found employment, but wound up either in a dead-end job or in one of the thousands of on-the-job classes to master the basic skills that they should have developed in high school. And, contrary to popular mythology, this is not a problem limited to the graduates of decaying urban school districts who enter four-year colleges. As a recent Washington Post report pointed out, even in wealthy suburban school districts like Montgomery County, Maryland, many of the graduates who enter the local community college end up in remedial courses.

This issue of Thinking K-16 focuses on the changes we need to make in *both* higher education and K-12—in our standards, our assessments, and our graduation requirements—to turn this pattern around.

Our conclusion that current requirements ask way too little of high school students (and their teachers) may at first seem to put us at odds with some of our readers. Many of you are worried about getting your students to existing standards; the last thing you want to hear is that those standards are too low.

Before we begin, then, let us be clear about three matters:

- First, we are deeply aware that getting the signals straight—that is, the standards and assessments right—is only one small step toward our goal of improving student achievement and closing the gap between groups. Fixing the tests and other requirements, in other words, will not by itself fix the problem. Teachers and administrators will need lots of help in replacing outdated and low-level

continued next page

Inside Thinking K-16

➘ **"Murder is No Mystery"** This report by Public/Private Ventures gets to the basic causes of homicide in Philadelphia, and includes a very detailed assessment of numbers and facts.

➘ **"Leave No Child Behind"** The Children's Defense Fund's motto is so good George W. Bush snatched it for the name of his education platform.

Step Two: The Edit

Plan on writing a few drafts of the report so that you can go back and simplify and clarify your writing several times. No matter how brilliant and concise a writer you are, your work still needs editing. It may be hard to find someone who can really give your work a tough edit. But it's incredibly useful. Depending on how you set this project up, you may be the editor for someone else's writing, or you may be handing your first draft to a freelance editor. Whatever your system is, we highly recommend having a different person than the writer edit the piece.

Our approach to editing uses several different stages. One helpful way to think about the edit process is like a series of sieves with finer and finer mesh. At first, you deal with the biggest issues, and at the end of the process you focus on the nitpicky details and the niceties of good writing.

TOP EDIT

Begin with a content edit, focusing on the big ideas and concepts. As a reader, will you completely understand the situation, and are there examples that illustrate the problem? Do gaps in the logic leave you unconvinced of the conclusions? Do you think the recommendations will solve the problems? This stage of editing almost inevitably leads to more research and to some re-writing—often major re-organizing.

Keep in mind that tough edits, while hard on the ego, create good results. *The advice of an intelligent critic is invaluable.* One of the most important things to do at this point is to take a few steps back and make sure the draft answers the questions that any curious but uninformed person would want to know right away: Why does this issue matter? Who does it affect? How does it work? It's very easy to forget to address the simplest questions, and dive right into the insider stuff, leaving your readers behind.

This stage of editing can be a little overwhelming, but remember, unless you are completely happy with the ideas, examples and arguments within the report—and that is very, very rare—the writer is going to rework large sections of the text. So don't bother at this point to fix misspellings, misplaced commas, awkward introductions, etc. There's a good chance that sentence you finessed isn't going to be there in the next draft anyway.

REVIEW PROCESS

You'll want to go through several edits, but once the report has been edited and re-written once, you can get some broader feedback. Now is when you'll call upon some of those new friends you made during the interview process, and ask for their thoughts and their input. These people are a sample of the audience you'll be trying to sway with the final report—better to have an idea of what they think of your research, conclusions and recommendations now than after you've printed 3,000 copies and called a press conference.

Independence is the key to the success of Seattle's Northwest Environment Watch—and the nonprofit research center relies on a stringent review process to make sure its arguments are water-tight. They enlist between six and 30 reviewers for every project, fair-minded independent experts from the academic, policy and advocacy worlds. Although the group's aim is to promote a sustainable way of life in the Pacific Northwest, "we get some of our best feedback from conservative and libertarian perspectives," says research associate Joanna Lemly. "If you just talk with people who agree with you, you are missing a huge population of people you want to reach." The group uses the review process to vet their own work, making sure that it passes high standards for both logic and research.

Think about what you want from your reviewers before you enlist their help. Is this person ready and able to do a close read of how each of your sections works, or is he/she more appropriate for a general sense of it all? Be able to explain to others how you will use their comments, so that no misunderstandings arise. And before you start, think about what you will do if someone has a really big problem. You don't need to accept every criticism, but you should have an idea of what could change your mind about the various parts of the report.

You may want to limit how much work you are asking from reviewers by either giving them at least a few weeks to get back to you or by sending a very condensed version of the recommendations without all the background and context. If you are going to ask a group of ordinary people for input, you may want to invite them to a focus group instead of asking each one to read the whole document.

When the results are in, decide whose input to use and whose to shrug off. Listen to the critiques, but be prepared to stick to your guns. You don't have to please all your reviewers, as long as you give their criticisms a serious look. That said, at this point one of your reviewers will often point out a major hole in your argument or research. It can be devastating, but it's much better to catch the omission now than learn about it later from your critics on the Op-Ed page of your local paper. Just do the research you need to do to settle the question.

"[Because of the review process], there are things we've altered and omitted, and sometimes we've found that we did not know enough to make a claim," Northwest Environment Watch's Lemly says. For example, in one report on the region's electricity use, a reviewer pointed out that an incorrect assumption meant the use of fossil fuel was underreported. The new data required an entirely new set of figures and even changed some of the report's basic conclusions.

The beauty of this process is that people feel real ownership of the document when it's finished, because they directly influenced how it was created. And when they have buy-in, you can ask for help. For instance, if an assistant commissioner read a draft and gave suggestions, he probably will be willing to give it to the mayor's people to read with his endorsement. Or the

HOT TIP

Explain Your Mess

Be sure your reviewers know that the editing isn't done, so they aren't shocked that your "report" has grammatical and other minor errors (or that they aren't angry after wasting hours doing end-of-the-process proofreading).

head of the Chamber of Commerce might agree to be a source when you tell reporters which supporters to call for quotes.

During this stage, don't forget the home team: Be sure you understand your organization's internal review process. Who else needs to sign off? Does your board of directors need to see a draft before you publish? You probably don't want to add unnecessary editors to the process, but make sure everyone is on board, especially if your recommendations go beyond what your group has asked for in the past.

FINE TUNING

Now you're happy with what you're saying. Time to work on how you say it. This usually involves cutting, pasting and more rewriting. You might have the right pieces in the wrong order. Do they make sense and fit together? A lot of this stage also simply entails removing redundancies and unnecessary language.

If you're doing the fine tuning right, it doesn't come easy. For our 16-page reports, we'll typically spend at least two weeks working through this stage.

Next comes the final edit for language and tone. Here, especially, is where you should listen for awkward or confusing sentences or ideas. Some people like to read their drafts aloud, which can help identify where the writing gets sloppy or unclear.

Also make sure to scan over your document for self-righteousness or an unnecessarily alarmist tone. It can come across

INFORMATION

Display Copy

Headlines, sub-headlines, pull quotes, chart titles and captions are collectively known as "display copy," and they deserve your extra-special loving attention. These phrases should be sharp, focused, catchy and short. They draw people into the text.

Write your display copy with the assumption that most of your readers will never read your report's main text. (Unfortunately, that's probably true.) Someone should get your basic message just by skimming through all the display copy.

"You are trying to get the attention of someone who is looking to get to the heart of the matter quickly," says Alyssa Katz, editor of *City Limits* magazine. "Display copy should grab a reader in the gut with something they haven't thought of before. The world is complicated and policy solutions might not be simple. Display copy serves as a soundbite that brings readers into a more complicated analysis."

Later, all these textual elements will need to be proofread with special care. For some reason, they tend to attract typos, and they are also the first place your readers' eyes will go.

Pull quotes—a line or two excerpted from the main text and set in much larger typeface on the page—deserve their own special mention. A good pull quote is strongly written, immediately comprehensible yet intriguing, and less than 20 words. Generally, you want to use a pull quote adapted from the text on the same page, but don't be afraid to edit or abridge some of the text to make the words sound better. If you take a few minutes to glance at a couple of major magazines it won't take long to get an idea of how it's done.

The example on the opposite page, from the Annie E. Casey Foundation's publication *Advocasey* gives a good idea of how a collection of elegant display copy works. It both gives the reader an idea of the main concepts at a glance and breaks up what would otherwise have been a drab page.

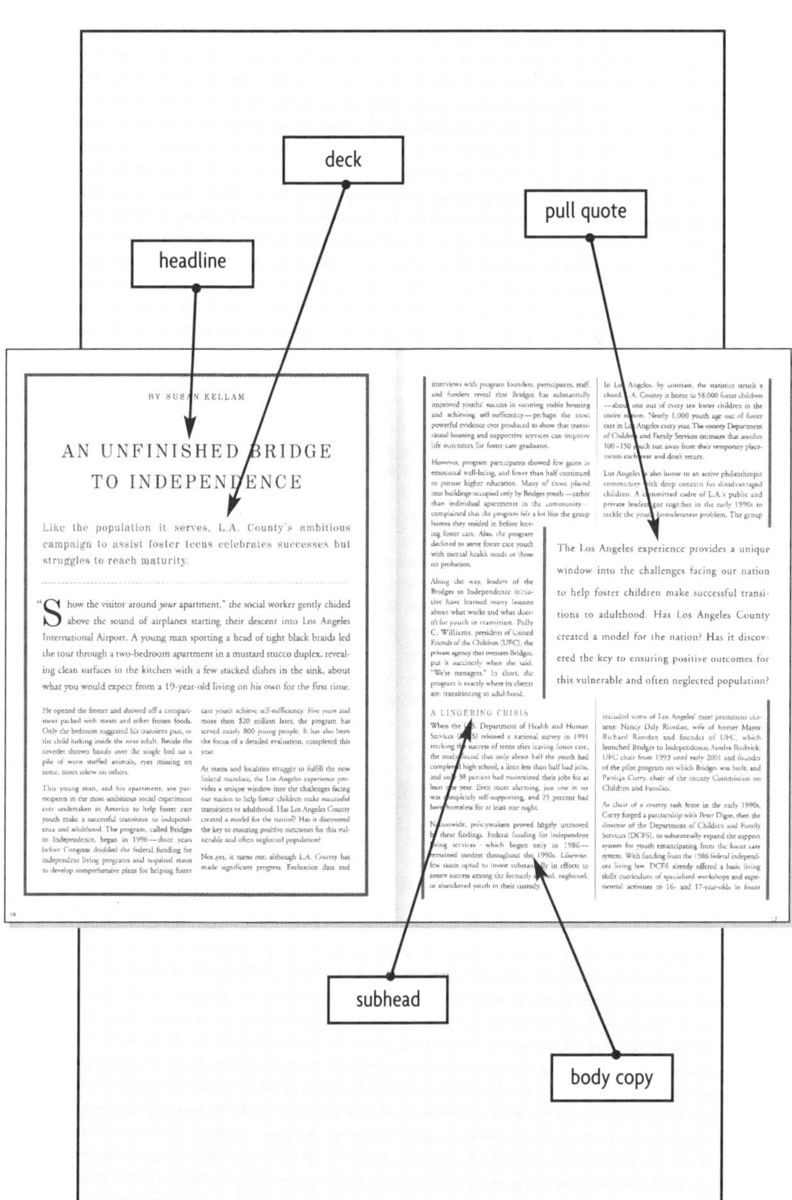
deck
pull quote
headline
BY SUSAN KELLAM
AN UNFINISHED BRIDGE TO INDEPENDENCE
Like the population it serves, L.A. County's ambitious campaign to assist foster teens celebrates successes but struggles to reach maturity.
"Show the visitor around *your* apartment," the social worker gently chided above the sound of airplanes starting their descent into Los Angeles International Airport. A young man sporting a head of tight black braids led the tour through a two-bedroom apartment in a mustard stucco duplex, revealing clean surfaces in the kitchen with a few stacked dishes in the sink, about what you would expect from a 19-year-old living on his own for the first time.
The Los Angeles experience provides a unique window into the challenges facing our nation to help foster children make successful transitions to adulthood. Has Los Angeles County created a model for the nation? Has it discovered the key to ensuring positive outcomes for this vulnerable and often neglected population?
A LINGERING CRISIS
subhead
body copy

as annoying or even silly. We once got a press release that announced a protest for a "Day of Perpetual Outrage." Allowing the facts to speak for themselves works better.

FINAL STEPS

At the end of the edit and into the design of the report, you should devote some time to fact-checking. If you want to be a stickler, get someone who has not been involved with the writing and editing process to cross-check and quickly re-report anything factual in your work—including spellings, the exact title of anyone who was quoted, dates and numbers, confirming any opinion or idea directly attributed to any person, etc. (Experienced fact checkers are a great asset here, and can work very quickly.) Or you may simply double-check your own work. Just make sure that someone takes time to do it—errors often creep in, and you don't want to make an embarrassing mistake.

Step Three: Report Design

Given how hard you've worked, you want to make sure it shows. A well-designed report will showcase all that hard labor. More importantly, good design makes the ideas more accessible and easier to read. Think classy and understated rather than pretty.

"People who take the time to make a good presentation often have better content. This notion that more sincere people don't have time to make things look good is not true," says Gail Nayowith, executive director with New York City's

Citizens' Committee for Children. "The effort has a value and is a reflection of the worth of the content."

DESIGN BASICS

You might want to hire a professional designer to create your report. If you do it yourself, we suggest you learn more about

RESOURCES

Design Winners

You'll have your own tastes for what you think a booklet should look like, but for simple, clean, sharp design, we admire the reports put out by these groups. You can see how their printed reports look by downloading pdf-formatted copies at their websites.

- Public/Private Ventures (www.ppv.org)
- FOMC Watch (www.fmcenter.org)
- Cato Institute (www.cato.org)
- The Annie E. Casey Foundation (www.aecf.org)

how graphic design works with some background reading on the basics. But even if you or your consultant is a design whiz, you might want to think about the following—reports have their own quirks just like any other medium.

Use design to make your point

Ask yourself, what do you want the reader to take away from your report? Your report doesn't have to look like a spread in *Vanity Fair*, but don't bury your ideas in long gray blocks of text, either. You should play up the three or four most significant points in the design with charts, sidebars and that

HOT TIP

Costs of the Report

For an 16-page report produced and printed in New York, we pay about:

$1,200 for design work

$3,800 for printing 4,000 copies in black and white

$650 for mailing house

$500 for third-class rate postage

$6,150 TOTAL

display copy. This can be especially useful to explain complex problems or processes. For example, in one of our *Child Welfare Watch* issues, we laid out a two-page flowchart of what a family goes through once they're in the legal system. The long, elaborate maze was more eloquent than any description we could give about how hard the system was to

WORKSHEET

Proofread Points

Proofreading is an editing task, but we suggest doing it at the very end of the design, when you can look at the text as it will appear in its final form. Nobody's perfect, but too many mistakes really detract from all the hard work you've put into creating a report, and last-minute adjustments are especially prone to error. Ask someone who hasn't read it before to proofread the whole thing, looking for typos, misspellings and inconsistencies.

Unfortunately, there are thousands of ways to have something go wrong. Here, however, are a few common typos and other mistakes:

- **Name check:** Double-check proper names, spellings and affiliations, and make sure they are spelled the same way through the whole document. There's no faster way to look bad than to misspell someone's name. And don't just leave it to your spell-check software. At *City Limits*, we once printed an issue in which New York City political operative Mike Long was inadvertently re-named "Mile Long." Whoops.
- **Acronym check:** Squint at the page. Does it look like a stew of abbreviations and capital letters? Replace every other reference to "the CIA" or "the UFO" with nouns like "the agency" or "the spacecraft."
- **Organization check:** Explain what groups do if it's not obvious. Don't just cite the findings of the American Industrial Hygiene Association without mentioning who they are and what makes them experts.

navigate (and it helped readers follow what we were referring to in different parts of the report).

Brand yourself

Anything you put out should have a recognizable style. You might bridle at the idea of applying an advertising concept like branding to public policy, but developing a consistent "look" for your documents is just one more way to get people to remember you. It doesn't have to be complex. We recommend that, at minimum, you use the same logo, font and cover design for all your reports.

Get some attention

Your first page should be designed so that someone can't help but read at least the first few paragraphs. You wrote a good lead, so make sure that it's eye-catching. We usually do this by using a larger font for the first couple lines of our introduction.

Keep that attention

Make sure the display text that you spent all that time agonizing over is cleanly presented and easily visible. Plan to have some kind of graphic element like a pull quote, sidebar or chart on every two-page spread, so that something catches the eye every time a reader turns the page.

Don't get too complicated

We all have access to dozens of fonts that can be bolded, underlined, offset and generally messed with any number of ways. Resist temptation. Keep the text design simple. Limit yourself to only a couple of fonts. Don't crowd too much text onto one page (700 words per page is a ballpark number).

Use color sparingly

This isn't an ad campaign for a new lipstick. You can do no wrong by sticking with black-and-white, but if you have a little money you may want to add color. It makes the document more enticing, but be careful—it can also make the report look goofy. Our house rule is that heavily reported investigative documents are printed in black and white, and more conceptual reports get small touches of subtle color.

WORKING WITH YOUR DESIGNER

Most people contract out their design work—it's a rare organization that keeps a designer on staff. To find a good designer, check out other reports that you like the looks of, and find out who those organizations hired. You can even farm out your design work to someone in New York or San Francisco, where the business is concentrated. (Another reason to be technologically up to speed!) We've found that each graphic artist has his or her own characteristic style, and the best way to make sure that your document looks the way you want it to is to choose a designer who has a style you already like.

Take a little time in the beginning to explain to your designer what you want. It really helps. If you're not sure how to describe the look you want, find a few other magazines or reports that you admire and show them to your designer. That said, trust in your designer to make the artistic decisions. Most professional designers have a pretty good sense of how to organize information.

You'll need to find a printer, too. Again, you can ask other policy organizations, or your designer may have a printer that he or she prefers to work with.

Design, like editing, is a back-and-forth process. Let your designer know that you'll want to go through a couple revisions before you finish. That's not an unreasonable request, but it's best to let your designer know from the beginning. As you look at the first draft, *be prepared to do a bit of production editing, to make chapters fit onto the page, sidebars bal-*

ance out throughout the report, etc. It doesn't have to be much, but you want someone who is familiar with the text and what you're trying to say to be making those calls.

From here, you and/or your designer will be sending out your beautifully designed, fascinating and powerful report to be printed, which generally takes somewhere between two to three weeks. Pat yourself on the back, but don't relax too much. There's some serious work that needs to get done before you can send out that report when it comes back.

CHAPTER SIX

Selling the Report

Selling the Report

You've worked hard to create solid, smart, accessible policy proposals. Now comes the fun part. It's time to sell.

In this stage, try to think like a player from a Madison Avenue ad agency, except that your product is in the public interest. You're going to package your work, gloss it up, put a nice big bow tie on it, and promote the hell out of it. You want the biggest audience that you can get. When lots of people listen to you, politicians and policymakers will take you seriously as well.

Marketing your work doesn't have to be sleazy. In fact, what really succeeds is a little bit of flash combined with a whole lot of doggedness and determination. Self-promotion may not come to you naturally, but remember that without plugging yourself and your work, it'll end up like so many other valuable policy proposals: ignored and forgotten. "We might release a report that is more than a hundred pages, but our work really begins after it is out the door," says Neil Mello.

Before you release your report, make sure you're prepared

with a clear message that takes into account the right context. While the report is at the printer, think through a strategy for its release and how you'll follow up. We'll give you some ideas

> Marketing your work doesn't have to be sleazy. In fact, what succeeds is a little bit of flash combined with a whole lot of doggedness and determination.

of how to get people thinking about—and talking about—your report, with a real emphasis on getting press. But it doesn't stop there, and we have some suggestions on other ways to use your report to affect change, too.

Step One: Prepare Your Message

You need to reach two audiences: the general public and policymakers. Policymakers are important because they make the laws and regulations that affect the issues you care about. The public, in turn, make the policymakers. You'll be aiming to convince both groups with different materials and events, but even when you're talking to policymakers, your arguments become stronger and more convincing in language that everyone can understand.

Seth Borgos of the National Campaign for Jobs and Income Support, a nonprofit that assists local efforts such as living wage campaigns, has a colleague with a "brother-in-law" test.

He calls his brother-in-law, a nice, regular guy with a mainstream perspective, and asks what he thinks of the ideas and phrases in his public policy agendas. If the brother-in-law understands what he's talking about and can discuss the issue with him, he knows it's ready for the general public. If his brother-in-law seems confused, he has more work to do.

If you don't have a brother-in-law, you can try out the same approach with a friend. Pick an intelligent, curious person who doesn't know anything about your work.

Just because your message is in universal language doesn't mean that you won't tinker with it to tailor it to different audiences. After all, talking policy with the lady down the street will be very different than talking to a government official who oversees a program. You should try to speak to both people in their own language. Similarly, when you start to do media work, you'll want to produce another variety of the same message, in order to get attention from the press.

CONSIDER THE CONTEXT

As you start to think about how to market your message, now's the time to take a closer look at the context. Keep current politics and social trends in mind. For example, if you know the mayor is running for governor and wants to associate himself with family-friendly policies, you might highlight the elements in your policy work that resonate with those themes. This is sheer political expediency: If the mayor thinks your ideas may help win him the governor's seat, he can be a crucial ally.

Last year, the Independent Press Association produced a

report on the influence and scope of New York City's largely unrecognized collection of more than 200 ethnic and community papers. The first press release they sent out "fell like a deadweight," says Abby Scher, the director of the IPA New York office. Then they wrote another release that talked about the report in regard to New York's 2000 Census data, which showed a massive influx of immigrants from around the globe. This time, they were written up in dozens of papers, including the *Boston Globe, Los Angeles Times, Newsday, PR Weekly* and *Crain's New York Business*.

You don't necessarily include context as an explicit part of your message. It might just be how you frame the issues. But however you handle it, talk that context over with your colleagues to make sure you that you are all of the same mind and coming from the same place.

DEVELOP YOUR POINTS

Within that context, name your key points. There shouldn't be more than a few of them, and they should fit neatly into no more than three sentences that explain what the policy change should be and why it needs to happen. These are the same ideas that helped guide you through writing and editing the report. Sharpen them, run them past your colleagues, revise them and use the brother-in-law test on them as well. Your report's executive summary is the short version of the whole story, and these points are the short version of the executive report.

The Correctional Association of New York's most recent campaign is against New York state's Rockefeller drug laws, a very strict set of rules that lock people up for a long time for having a small amounts of drugs. Their slogan, "Drop the Rock," is short and punchy, and the campaign is designed to work around three clear points:

1. At great expense to the taxpayer, these laws fill our prisons with non-violent offenders.
2. The laws are marked by racial bias.
3. Alternatives are available that save money and cut crime.

HOT TIP

A Few Pointed Words

Be able to explain your report in 25 words or less. Yes, it will be simplistic. But initially, you need to get people interested, and there's no better way to do it than with a couple of pithy, snappy lines.

The campaign touches upon some powerful themes—fairness, government waste and safety—and it's very easy to understand. Just like a pull quote gives a reader the idea of what they'll learn if they read the text, a good set of key points gives anyone who hears them the basic thrust of your argument and makes them want to know more.

PREPARE YOUR SUPPORTERS

Before you release your document, line up your allies. This is important: The more people you have ready to support you, the better.

First, figure out who can turn your recommendations into reality, going back to that long list of people you've been in in contact with. This is when all that earlier work of developing a huge network of sources really pays off. Now, right there in your database, you know exactly who matters, what they think and where to find them.

While the document is at the printer, call the people who are potential allies to see if they are willing to lend support. They might help craft legislation, testify at hearings, distribute the report at meetings they routinely attend or talk to the press. Again, the people who helped give feedback are especially invested in the product.

Give supporters a copy of the report shortly before you release it. If you expect some of them to talk to reporters, help respond to press calls, be part of a press conference or speak in other public forums, make sure they know your major points and agree with them. More prosaically, make sure they'll be available and ready to respond right away.

Step Two: The Press

One well-placed newspaper article or TV story can sometimes do more to change policy than six months' worth of coalition building, advocating and schmoozing. *If you're small as David, and your policy target's Goliath, the media is your slingshot.* For better or for worse, the press is your best chance to broadcast your message and force that big monster to listen to you.

"Press coverage is the coin of the advocacy realm," says John

Kaehny, executive director of Transportation Alternatives in New York City, a group that advocates for cyclists and pedestrians. "We drop everything and respond immediately to requests for comment. If we must, we do the research and sometimes have practically written the story."

Kaehny notes that one newspaper story did what activists and planners could not: improve safety in Herald Square on 34th Street. "There was a two-year planning process by the City Department of Transportation to improve the safety of the area for cyclists and pedestrians. But Macy's wanted to kill it. So we added drama, intrigue and life and death to a seemingly boring planning process and we pitched it to the *Times*. They loved it and wrote a huge puff piece on how fantastic the pedestrian improvements were and how much better life would be around 34th Street. When that piece ran, the DOT got the courage to push it through. [Without the article], it would have been stalled or killed by opposition from Macy's. Now, it had to happen, or the mayor would be embarrassed. With one story we pushed through a major plan in Midtown Manhattan."

Solid work, an interesting story and a clear, focused message take you far with the press. If you've followed our advice, you already have a product that reporters will like. If you're persistent about selling it, you'll succeed.

How the press present issues has a tremendous influence on public opinion, determining not just what people know about an issue but also what they think about what they know. That knife cuts both ways, though. So a lot of what follows is about care and feeding of reporters—what they look for, how to get them excited about a story, how to control

INFORMATION

What Reporters Really Want

Many reporters depend on a handful of reliable sources—people they can call at the last minute who will fill them in on the background of an issue, put fast-breaking news in context and connect them with other knowledgeable people. If you can play this role, and maintain an ongoing relationship with one or more reporters, your perspective will often be the one that winds up in the newspaper or on TV. What's even better is your name often won't be attached to that viewpoint. If that seems counterintuitive (don't you want everyone to know you?), consider this: your views will seep into the framing and context of the story, which gives you deeper control over how the issue is presented—because it'll be harder to identify and challenge your perspective.

the way the information is presented.

Always remember, you don't just want to be in the paper, you want to be one of the stories readers remember. We're all bombarded with information. Policymakers are even worse off, since they are the constant target of groups wanting to change public policy. Figure out which words will stick, and which ideas and stories will stay in people's minds. And send your message as many ways as you can. It increases the chances that some of it will get through.

There are literally hundreds of sources of advice for nonprofits on how to "sell" a message and how to get coverage for your story—a quick web search will give you several quality ones. We like the media advocacy advice at Center for Community

Change (communitychange.org). We won't go through all of that again. But we will tell you about our own experiences.

FAIR WARNING

Working with the media is risky. For one thing, you have lots of competition. Offering good information and developing relationships with reporters helps, but a last-minute fire or political scandal can always push your story into the dustbin.

On top of that, reporters have prejudices just like everyone else—try as hard as you might, the story may wind up being more about the reporter's opinions than about your agenda or even some balanced view of the truth. For example, in the wake of the September 11th attacks, CNN called the Independent Press Association, wanting to be put in touch with representatives from the ethnic press. However, the producers weren't interested in the views of the city's immigrant communities. Rather, they wanted to report on false rumors being published in New York's ethnic papers. Not exactly what the IPA was trying to promote. And even when the reporter is on your side, her editor might not think the story is sexy or jazzy enough.

Of course, corporate agendas and blind prejudices of all kinds can influence and even distort the way a media outlet approaches a story. The fact is, you don't control what gets printed. You also can't take full responsibility for your press. (Sometimes that is a good thing to fall back on, as when a political bigwig doesn't like the story that mentions your work.)

More common than prejudice is small-mindedness. Believe it

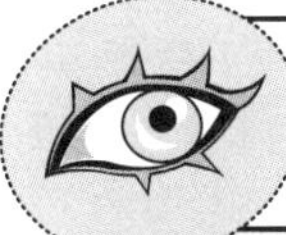

C A S E S T U D Y

That's Not What I Meant

We weren't unhappy at all when we were slammed as "a grouplet with a fax machine" in the pages of the *New York Post* (see below). After all, the paper is the city's most powerful purveyor of conservative dogma. But rather than engage in a real debate about our report on the role of race in the city's foster care system, the editorial board simply accused us of throwing the race card. The press doesn't always play along.

EDITORIAL

June 28, 199

SMEARING CHILDREN'S SERVICES

New York is an amazing place. Any liberal or left-wing grouplet with a fax machine can put out a "study" charging racism/sexism/any-ism and it gets written up in the papers as if it should be taken seriously.

Case in point: Something calling itself Child Welfare Watch last week put forth a study purporting to show racism in the city's foster-care system. It claimed, among other things, that black children are twice as likely as white children to be removed from homes where they are abused or neglected. It also claimed that black children stay longer in foster care than whites; that the number of relatives used as foster parents has declined; and that parents are not adequately represented in Family Court.

The Administration for Children's Services, which Commissioner Nicholas Scoppetta is doing his manly best to straighten out with precious little thanks from anyone, has responded to a number of these points.

First, he points out that kinship placements are actually up by 8 percent. The total number is down as children placed in foster care in the 1980s age out of the system.

As for the alleged lack of "adequate" legal representation, it is a liberal golden oldie that everybody who doesn't have an O.J.-style "dream team" at their disposal was not"adequately" represented. The fact is that representation is provided for every indigent parent at every initial court appearance. And no child is removed from the custody of a parent without the approval of a Family Court judge at a proceeding at which all parties are represented by counsel.

As to why a higher proportion of black children end up in foster care than Latino or white children, ACS offers no opinion. But we can submit some possibilities.

Illegitimacy, for example, is a contributing factor to kids ending up in foster care. And the rate of illegitimate births among blacks nationally is around 70 percent (compared with about 25 percent for whites and 43 percent for Hispanics). We don't know what the black rate is in New York City, but we doubt it is below the national level.

Throw in drug abuse and criminal activity, both of which disproportionately afflict the black community, as well as a foster-care system that functions, in effect, as a form of supplemental-income for many blacks, and the reasons for more blacks in foster care become manifest.

Given these realities, it is not at all clear that placing more black children in foster care is evidence of racism. Indeed, it could be quite the contrary.

or not, the real risk you run is not that your issue will get biased coverage. It's that it will never see the light of day at all. More and more, reporters and their editor bosses only want the most straightforward stories: Highway Construction Delayed. Candidate Promises Less Crime. Homeless Shelter Plan Angers Neighbors. And so forth. A lot of public policy issues are complicated and technical, without a clear winner or loser, and are therefore harder to tell in rigid journalistic formats. That's why the more compelling and convincing your message is, and the more sources, data and anecdotes you have to back it up, the easier it will be for a reporter to adapt in his or her own story. Often, these reporters are churning out three or four stories a day. By doing a lot of their work for them, you make it that much more likely that your perspective and your opinions will be in the newspaper or on TV tomorrow.

LINE UP THE REPORTERS

Presswork is about relationships. Broadcasting your press release is not as useful as a targeted, personal approach. Rather than faxing every media person in the city, get to know four or five reporters. Most daily reporters are hungry for strong news, and they're all vying to get their story on the front page.

In your research, you tracked local coverage and figured out who generally covers your issues. That's the best place to start—those people will be most likely to report on you. Use that list, and take into account which media outlets your policy targets pay attention to, including:

- Local television news programs

- Local morning shows
- Cable and public access television shows
- Big daily newspapers
- Weekly newspapers and magazines, including alternative papers
- Chains that serve a geographic area
- Small local papers
- Regional monthly magazines
- Radio stations that cover news
- Public and college radio stations
- Websites that cover local issues
- Talk radio—hosts are often desperate for issues, and it's a great way to practice explaining and defending your views before an audience.

Go first to the outlets that are already strong on the issue. If you don't know who covers the topic, ask around. Call your colleagues who regularly get press coverage and ask them who does a good job and who they respect. For more names, call a newspaper's metro desk—or a television station's assignment desk—and ask for the assigning editor. Explain that you have a press event coming up, or that you want to talk to the appropriate journalist about a report you are releasing.

Once you've figured out who covers your issues, call that person all the time—when you hear good gossip, a particularly compelling individual story, or when an important change is coming up in the issue you cover. If a reporter thinks that your story or contacts will make her famous, you won't be able to get rid of her.

RESOURCES

For More On the Press

There are plenty of books, articles and Web sites with good advice for policy groups who want to entice the press. Here are some favorites:

- "Making Policy, Making Change: How Communities Are Taking Law into Their Own Hands," a book by Makani Themba Nixon, is aimed at grassroots organizers. Of particular help are discussions of how you can address issues of consistent racial and corporate bias in the media.
- The site for the Center for Community Change has a short guide with helpful information on how to develop advocacy agendas relevant to low-income communities, as well as good articles on how to work with the media (commchange.org).
- The Chicago-based Community Media Workshop works with community and civic organizations around media issues, and their website (newstips.org) has some very good links.
- Princeton University's Project for Excellence in Journalism sponsors a good site for discussion and analysis of bias in media with clear descriptions of how reporters "frame" and interpret news stories (journalism.org/framing.html).

EXCLUSIVES, FOR GOOD AND EVIL

Why give exclusives? A few reasons: It's the closest thing to a guarantee that you'll get coverage. Reporters like scooping their competitors by getting to a good story first. You may want to reward a reporter who has covered your work in the past, and who you trust not to distort your message. An exclusive can also assure coverage of a specialized or unusual story that might not otherwise get any press.

That said, most reporters will not be interested in an exclusive unless you have truly surprising or powerful news. And granting an exclusive is a political act that can spark resentment from other reporters. If your story comes out as an exclusive before you hold a press conference, it's likely that nobody else will attend the conference because the story is already old news. On the other hand, if the story is really big, that exclusive coverage could actually attract the interest of other outlets.

THE MANY FLAVORS OF MEDIA

Newspapers and TV cover the same story in different ways. Don't pitch an in-depth analytical piece to a television news show. By the same token, don't try to sell a visually engaging protest to a radio station.

Certain media may be a more natural fit for you. For example, we find that television can be hard for policy stories, because it's difficult to get into complex issues on TV. Often, the piece turns into a sob story about one person's troubles with, say, getting into community college, and leaves out the more complicated systemic issues. On the other hand, TV is immediate, direct and reaches a huge audience. Human interest stories can be very powerful if you can help the reporter find "sympathetic" subjects who will go on the air.

Even though it may make you cringe to take this approach, someone's painful personal story is often the most obvious 'peg' for the story. For their work to increase public funding for mental health care, Citizens' Committee for Children worked with a television reporter to find parents who would talk about their mentally ill children. It was very difficult to find willing subjects, but the TV station helped by not using peoples' last names and by electronically blurring their faces. The final two-part series was very powerful and emotional, a unique part of a lobbying campaign that really drove the message home that this problem needed to be addressed.

In print media, your issue may fit in one of many sections of the newspaper. Will it focus on a single example of the problem–looking at one family or one company affected by bad public policies? Is it a story for the business section that will talk about a number of companies? Is it a story about a relationship–like that of a health insurance company to an individual who is ill?

If the larger outlets aren't interested, or you think the story will sell best to smaller town or neighborhood-focused places, go there instead. If you're not yet comfortable with your pitch, it can help to approach the smaller newspapers and cable television stations first—they will give you a little more time to make your point and are more forgiving if you're awkward or muddled.

You don't have to choose one type of press over the other, since you can sell the same story more than once. Usually, print reporters compete with other print reporters, and likewise with TV. That means that just because the story has already been "done," if it was in another media format, a reporter may still want to cover it.

Also, big media fish feed off the little ones. Reporters all read, watch and listen to one another's work. If the *Washington Post* isn't interested in your story, it's worth talking to smaller outlets. You can follow the same food chain that the media does: start local, then pitch that story to the more powerful newspapers, and from there move to television. Keep in mind John Kaehny's advice: "We target print media because, frankly, TV is moronic—and they follow print anyway."

RELEASING THE DOCUMENT

With all this in mind, you need to decide how you're going to release your document. During the week before the report is back from the printer, we usually come up with a pitch, refine it, and then reach out to a couple of reporters who we think will be interested. In a brief phone call, we explain what the report says, why it is newsworthy, and what kind of story could be written about its findings. We generally start at the top, with a reporter at the outlet we'd most like to have cover us—often, *The New York Times*. We might offer an exclusive to that reporter first and send him or her an advance copy of the report. If, in a couple of days, he or she isn't interested, we move down the list.

Exclusives are somewhat rare, so don't worry if nobody takes you up on your offer. You're not done yet. On the day you release the report, fax a press release at 8:30 in the morning to a broader list of reporters you've targeted. Then call within an hour and give a prepared pitch: just two or three sentences with your name and organization and the basics of the major report you just released. Did they get the fax? If not, make sure you have the right number and fax again. If they did, but aren't interested, ask why and if there's someone else who you should send it to at the paper. And if they say they might use it—the most common answer in our experience—call

back in a few hours, this time with new goodies: the numbers of a few allies to talk with, a great example of someone who is hurt by the current situation, a person in the mayor's office who could be quoted on the subject.

If it sounds like a lot of work, it is. But just sending out a fax and leaving it at that is almost guaranteed to fail. After all the work you put into the report, this day of cold calls is a small price to pay to get your ideas out. And as you build a reputation and get to know reporters, it gets much easier.

PRESS RELEASES

There are a lot of good books that explain how to write a press release, so suffice it to say the release should be short and well-edited—no more than a page—and sent to the right editors and reporters. If the releases are well-written, some

HOT TIP

And Now a Word From Our Sponsor

Whether you're doing a television interview or calling a reporter to pitch your report, don't forget to mention who you are and what your group does. "People often describe what they do, not who they are. So people will say, 'We fight for equity and housing and community gardens' and on and on. Just say who you are in one sentence," suggests Neil Mello of MassINC. "We say, 'We are a nonpartisan think tank focusing on issues important to the middle class.' If they want to know more, they'll ask."

media outlets will simply cut and paste your words and quotes directly into their story. (Good reporters call those people "hacks," but they are part of the business, too.)

If nobody responds to your press release, don't despair. It's just the beginning of your efforts. Reporters will be more likely to remember you and pay attention the next time you send one out.

THE PRESS CONFERENCE

Press conferences are a relatively efficient way to build excitement and get your message across to a large audience of reporters. You can add drama to the press conference by holding it somewhere relevant to the topic (A garbage dump? A port? A senior center?), or someplace reporters will want to visit. Part of the excitement comes from having a group of people there to listen to you, so if not many people show up, it can be an anticlimax.

Generally, we send advance copies of the report to press that express some interest in coming. That makes for a better conference, since they'll be more prepared and think of more interesting questions.

You'll want a few different people to speak at a press conference, which will also draw more press. Typically that would include someone affected by the policy you want changed, an independent expert and a practitioner or professional in the field. Try to avoid surprises through careful planning and good preparation of your speakers. While you can't control what people say, you should be clear with them about what you're asking of them, and even practice with anyone who isn't used to speaking before groups.

Someone who has personal experience with the issue you've written about, and who hasn't spoken to the press before, may need some coaching. Sit down with him or her before the conference and find a few concrete points that she or he will want to touch on. Develop them and write them down together, and let the person know what their time limit will be. (Inexperienced people tend to ramble.) Work out a way for that person to tell his or her own personal story and connect it to your larger policy points in a way that isn't stigmatizing or exploitative. It's their story, but you should help them chart the course.

BE A GOOD SOURCE

Getting an interview isn't the end of getting the word out. You want to be a good source. If you're talking about an interesting current issue or telling a story that's never been told, it doesn't take much to become a good spokesperson. Keep these ideas in mind—whether you're talking about your report or being called out of the blue to comment on a topic you're familiar with.

Speak clearly and succinctly

Find the balance between saying too much and saying too little. Don't drone on and on, trying to get in every last piece of information. As with writing your report, practice conveying the whole issue in simple language.

Michelle Yanche of the Neighborhood Family Services Coalition in New York recommends a post-mortem critique to sharpen your press skills. "There's no substitute for watching yourself and listening to yourself to improve your own media skills. Actively seek critiques from colleagues—as painful as that is. For me, it's a struggle to fight my own propensity to be very detail-oriented, and give too much information. When I speak spontaneously, I tend to ramble," she says. "Some people are naturals at this. It's a great lesson watching someone who's naturally highly quotable."

Be quick

Respond immediately to requests for comment and respect reporter's deadlines. "Our nimbleness is a big plus. The older and bigger groups just do not respond in time. They take forever to respond and have to go through the hierarchy of checking in with the president to see if it fits their official stance, etc." says John Kaehny of Transportation Alternatives.

These days, most print reporters have afternoon or evening deadlines; radio and TV reporters may need to talk to you within an hour or two. If you can't get back to a reporter immediately, you will lose your opportunity to comment.

Be honest and straightforward

Be upfront about where you're coming from—including your biases—and reporters will think of you as a credible source of information. But also find a way to mention all the different stakeholders you've spoken with—not just environmental advocates, for instance, but companies, academics, unions, economic development experts and lawmakers on both sides of the aisle. Don't parrot a party line. Talk your issue over; don't just issue a statement.

RESOURCES

The Secrets of Secrecy

"Off-the-record" means your comments may be anonymously quoted, whereas "on deep background" means that whatever you tell the reporter is not to appear in print at all. If you choose to talk anonymously, you absolutely must clarify this distinction at the beginning of the conversation. The rules of reporting hold that there are no "take-backs" in interviews. If you tell a reporter something and later decide you don't want to be quoted, you can't announce after the fact that it was on background.

Make your message nuanced and interesting

You should try to say something that no one else is saying, and convey the subtleties and complexities of the issue. If you present the issue as black and white—your position is right, and everyone else is wrong—then you may attract some attention just for being strident, but you will end up being pigeonholed. Press people may call you because they know exactly what you are going to say and they just want to hear you say it so they can quote you. You'll get more calls, though, if people expect your take on an issue to be deep and complex. That way, they can use your expertise to help them figure out what they should write. Stay provocative and you'll be better able to control the direction of the conversation and the debate.

Be up front

Acting as a public policy advocate means taking a stand, so speak as though anything you say might be quoted. You can ask to speak "on deep background" and not be quoted or cited as a source, but don't do that unless you really must. It's not in keeping with this kind of public policy campaign, and it can be risky—misunderstandings happen.

Connect reporters to other good sources

Even if you know a lot about the topic, you should have other sources available to back you up or to give another perspective. If you don't know about the specific issue he or she is interested in, tell the reporter who does. (That way, you'll make sure that you are the first person the reporter will turn to for information.) Most importantly, if you focus on a social issue and you want press attention, be prepared to help a reporter find an ordinary person who is coping with this issue—especially for TV. Chances are that the reporter will be more interested in talking to and quoting that person than you, even if you brought the issue to light.

Build relationships

Invest your time to educate a reporter you respect on an issue. It will pay off in the form of high-quality, in-depth coverage. And give reporters feedback—congratulate them on good work and alert them politely to mistakes, oversights and inaccuracies in their work. More than anything else, keep in touch.

Step Three: Beyond the Press

We've talked a lot about working the press because that's the main strategy for our small organization to have a big impact. But not every report we produce gets the kind of press we'd like. What happens if nobody pays attention? If you get minor media coverage—or none at all—and nobody besides your mom calls to say congratulations, you have to start reaching out to those people yourself.

Even when you do make the front page of the local paper, you may not be satisfied. Press is a tool, not an end unto itself, and if your goals haven't been met through of the publicity you garnered, then you may want to keep the pressure on. For most of our reports at the Center, we use at least a few of the following strategies to keep our issue in front of policymakers.

REPORT MAILINGS

Send your report out with an introductory letter to the people who are interested in the issue or who have some control over it. And because of your database, you can quickly get your report directly in the hands of the several hundred people that matter the most. This one is almost a no-brainer: You printed hundreds of copies of the report, now get them to the people who can help institute you recommendations.

For the core of our mailing list, we now send every report without a letter—they just know it's the latest from the Center. For people interested in a specific topic, we usually include a brief note introducing ourselves and mentioning the highlights and any actions we're hoping to come from its release. If there's a specific campaign underway on the issue, give a Website or phone number to get involved.

LET'S HAVE A MEETING

A few years ago, we released a report showing that even

though New York City had the highest density of prominent biomedical research centers in the country, it had no biotech industry to speak of. *The New York Times* gave our report major coverage and continued to follow up on the issue. Within a few weeks, the state Comptroller mentioned the topic in a speech and then-Senate candidate Hillary Rodham Clinton rewrote her campaign speech to include a call for more biotech industry in the region. The head of the city's Chamber of Commerce was also interested, and convened other businesses to set up biotech incubators in the city.

But if the *Times* hadn't been interested, or if nobody had read the article, we would have started by lobbying some of the same people. We probably would have called the head of the Chamber of Commerce, and asked to schedule a meeting to discuss our findings. We would have brought a few smart experts to that meeting—powerful leaders of biomedical institutions, if they were available, or the CEO of a small biotech company that had to move to New Jersey because of poor business conditions in the city. We would have called the Economic Development committee chair in the City Council, the mayor's business development staff, or anyone else we could think of who might be in a position to do something about the problems we'd uncovered.

These meetings might not be as much fun as being quoted by reporters, but they pay off. They must be arranged with care—some people won't be interested unless others have signed on, others won't agree to see you without an introduction, still others get upset if you don't meet with them first. Meeting by meeting and discussion by discussion, you can enlist people in your cause so that your message becomes a

movement. It's a time-consuming process, and it can be frustrating, since not all of these meetings will be productive. But to keep your research and ideas from sitting on a shelf, you need to talk to people.

We'll leave it there, because anything else we could tell you about this kind of advocacy is no different from what dozens of other books tell you. Remember, however, that you don't necessarily need to create a coalition or grassroots movement. You just need to convince people with the power to make changes that your ideas are worthwhile.

LETTERS TO THE EDITOR

This is a quick, inexpensive way to reach a lot of people, and will help raise the profile of your issue. Every newspaper runs some letters as a sounding board for public opinion. Write short and to the point—the less editing required, the better. Express strong opinions and if you can, tailor your letter to either complement or respond to the paper's editorial slant—whether conservative, liberal, intellectual or populist.

When the Idaho Community Action Network (ICAN) wanted to change state policies on publicly funded health insurance, members wrote editorial letters using a script that delivered the message, "Invest in the future of our children by funding health insurance coverage." "We had our members publishing letters in local newspapers all over the state. Any time that happens in a smaller state, the larger papers feel compelled to cover the story," says LeeAnn Hall, who organized the campaign with the Northwest Federation of Community Organizations. And in the end, the state legislature funded the program.

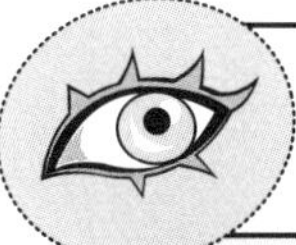

CASE STUDY

Dear Editor

When the Citizens' Committee for Children sent this letter to *The New York Times* last year, it went into more detail than the paper would print. But the language was clear enough that the editors could pick the points they felt were most important.

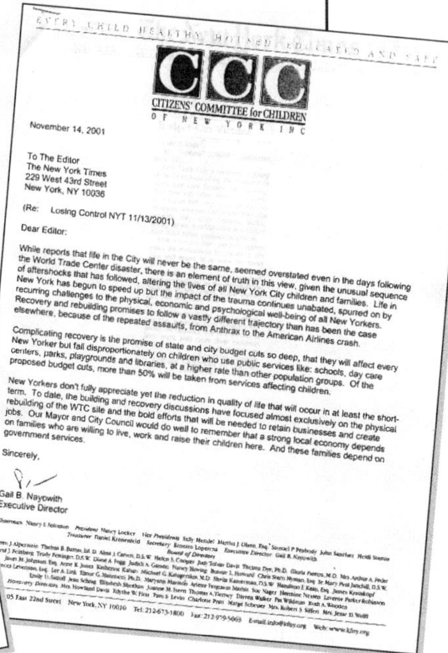

EVERY CHILD HEALTHY, HOUSED, EDUCATED AND SAFE

CCC
CITIZENS' COMMITTEE for CHILDREN
OF NEW YORK INC

November 14, 2001

To The Editor
The New York Times
229 West 43rd Street
New York, NY 10036

(Re: Losing Control NYT 11/13/2001)

Dear Editor:

While reports that life in the City will never be the same, seemed overstated even in the days following the World Trade Center disaster, there is an element of truth in this view, given the unusual sequence of aftershocks that has followed, altering the lives of all New York City children and families. Life in New York has begun to speed up but the impact of the trauma continues unabated, spurred on by recurring challenges to the physical, economic and psychological well-being of all New Yorkers. Recovery and rebuilding promises to follow a vastly different trajectory than has been the case elsewhere, because of the repeated assaults, from Anthrax to the American Airlines crash.

Complicating recovery is the promise of state and city budget cuts so deep, that they will affect every New Yorker but fall disproportionately on children who use public services like: schools, day care centers, parks, playgrounds and libraries, at a higher rate than other population groups. Of the proposed budget cuts, more than 50% will be taken from services affecting children.

New Yorkers don't fully appreciate yet the reduction in quality of life that will occur in at least the short-term. To date, the building and recovery discussions have focused almost exclusively on the physical rebuilding of the WTC site and the bold efforts that will be needed to retain businesses and create jobs. Our Mayor and City Council would do well to remember that a strong local economy depends on families who are willing to live, work and raise their children here. And these families depend on government services.

Sincerely,

Gail B. Nayowith
Executive Director

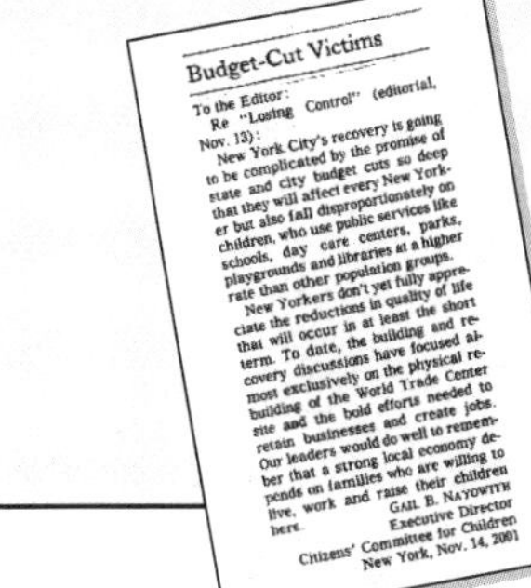

Budget-Cut Victims

To the Editor:

Re "Losing Control" (editorial, Nov. 13):

New York City's recovery is going to be complicated by the promise of state and city budget cuts so deep that they will affect every New Yorker but also fall disproportionately on children, who use public services like schools, day care centers, parks, playgrounds and libraries at a higher rate than other population groups.

New Yorkers don't yet fully appreciate the reductions in quality of life that will occur in at least the short term. To date, the building and recovery discussions have focused almost exclusively on the physical rebuilding of the World Trade Center site and the bold efforts needed to retain businesses and create jobs. Our leaders would do well to remember that a strong local economy depends on families who are willing to live, work and raise their children here.

GAIL B. NAYOWITH
Executive Director
Citizens' Committee for Children
New York, Nov. 14, 2001

PUBLIC SERVICE ANNOUNCEMENTS

PSAs take your message to a large audience, which is good if what you want to say is relevant and interesting to a lot of people. Besides local TV and radio stations, you can also try banner ads on websites. Be sure you've targeted the right audience, though, because it's a tremendous amount of work to produce the spots and find the outlets that will run them for free. Local cable stations may be willing to help you produce a spot which you can then take elsewhere. Television and radio

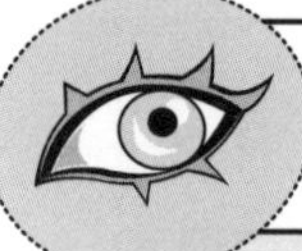

CASE STUDY

Wish You Were Here

In a recent campaign about affordable child care, the Citizens' Committee for Children of New York added another layer to its typical postcard campaign. Instead of simply asking people to sign their names, the card included a few blanks that required the sender to look at an attached map to see CCC's calculation of how many families in the neighborhood were lacking child care. It wasn't a big deal, but it did require that people read through the material and give the issues a few moments' thought. "It created a different level of consciousness not only for the public, but also for the agency that received the postcards," says Gail Nayowith, the group's executive director. "From the perspective of shaping public opinion, that was a big step forward for us."

CHILD CARE
the Family Life Issue in New York City

WHAT YOU CAN DO

Child Care: the Family Life Issue in New York City

Dear Mayor Giuliani,

The supply of quality, affordable child care falls far short of what working families need to live and work in New York City. Please use all available funds to fill the child care gap by:

- Ensuring that quality early childhood learning experiences are available for every young child.
- Developing a child care capacity expansion plan to meet the unmet need in city neighborhoods.
  In my Community District #______, there are_______ children age 0-5 years in need of child care.

Name ______________________________

Address ______________________________

City/State/Zip______________________________

stations automatically run PSAs, but, depending on your media market, your ad may only be seen by a few insomniacs. Consider if it's worth the effort.

PAID ADVERTISING

Paid ads can be very effective. They can also be very expensive, so weigh the cost. Is the magazine you're considering read by the general public or just by government officials? (Depending on your goal, either answer could be right for you.) Does a radio station have good news analysis and are its listeners likely to make a phone call for more information? Is there a local paper in the district of the legislator you most want to reach? When you pay for ads, the costs add up very quickly, so always be sure your message is focused to get to the right people.

"SEND A MESSAGE" CAMPAIGNS

If your message is focused on a specific, timely problem or proposal, you can try to quickly educate people and urge them to take action right away. Perhaps the deadline for the legislature to pass the budget is coming up soon. Postcards pre-addressed to policymakers are effective because they are specific and concrete ("vote no" or "vote yes") and they don't require too much effort on the part of the people sending them. Plus, they're a tangible reminder of public opinion.

But a postcard campaign does require some fast work on your part–design, printing and mailing—and again, you need a good database of contacts. They're most successful when you have a specific problem, a clear target to address them to, and a short, well-defined message.

Asking supporters to make telephone calls also works, though you can't control what people say. It also costs your supporters more money, and requires more effort. Email messages are generally less effective than telephone calls, letters or postcards, for the same reason that they are so popular: It's very easy to get them started and circulated—and legislators know it.

PUBLIC FORUMS

Policy forums and conferences reach a more select audience–the professionals and policymakers whose support you most want. By hosting a forum where people can hear experts talk about the issue, you can create an interesting and substantive discussion, give people access to the best thinkers, build a community of people, and highlight issues you've raised in your report.

Good public forums aren't just a celebration of your report. They spark a worthwhile public discussion. Unlike a press conference, you want people with different opinions there, and you want those differences to come out in the discussion. It's better for you if some people disagree with your conclusions and recommendations. The program will be livelier.

The most common response we hear from people who go to forums and conferences is, "It was nice, but I didn't learn anything new." Just by virtue of the speakers you invite to your forum, people should look at the invitation and say, "I might learn something if I go to this." We get standing-room only audiences at many of our events, and that's because they're not a series of testimonies about how clever we are. Because we have enough faith in our research and our ideas, we think that anyone who attends our events with an open mind will agree that our perspective makes sense.

TECHNOLOGY

Thanks to the information revolution, you have many ways to broadcast your message. Given the pace of development, we won't try to give timely technology advice here, aside from pointing out that you should stay up to date.

Regardless of the media you choose—listserves, faxes, even telephone calls—*don't clog up the information highway.* This is especially true with email and other electronic communications. It's hard to resist the temptation to forward all kinds of petitions and news alerts to everyone on your list. But don't. When you send out irrelevant information all the time, people stop paying attention. Be protective of your subscribers. Keep your content focused and only bring in other issues if they are directly relevant.

THE CLEVER PROTEST

The picket line, shouting crowd and civil disobedience are all time-honored ways to attract attention to your cause. Again, many books do a better job than we could of describing how to use protests to move your agenda. However, we just want to make a quick case for stunts.

New York City's community gardeners have mounted a variety of clever high-profile demonstrations in order to preserve the hundreds of small gardens that neighborhood people have started in vacant lots. The campaign got an enormous amount of press—and eventually attracted a celebrity benefactor—in part because the protests were always witty and original, virtually guaranteeing them heavy media coverage and winning a lot of public support.

The gardeners led spring parades with enormous dragonfly stilt puppets and little children dressed as flowers and bees (which television cameras loved). Some of their other actions were downright mischievous, like one in which activists placed false bids at an auction in which garden lots were being sold off. At another, they released thousands of crickets inside the auction hall during the sale. It should be noted, however, that at the same time, other garden groups were doing the more conventional work of gathering signatures, lobbying politicians and trying to work out a deal.

MEASURING PUBLIC OPINION

A final word on pushing your report. As your campaign unfolds, you're probably going to wonder how well you're doing in getting the public on your side. But public opinion is murky territory, hard to decipher. However, there are some tools that will help you figure out if you've reached people.

Polling is the most accurate method, but it is expensive. Instead, you might want to consider some seat-of-the-pants polls that can give you at least an idea of how well you're getting your message out.

- Ask for feedback or discussion on your website. If your materials all give your web address and mention that more information is available on-line, you can even use the number of hits your site gets as a rough measure of how many people are interested.

- Ask your peers if they are talking about your ideas. And try to find people you trust to give you an honest answer—"Oh, yeah, we talk about them all the time," might not count. Of course, other people interested in your policy area aren't a representative sample of the general public, but they are a sample of people who spend time thinking about and making decisions about your topic. Sometimes public opinion doesn't mean people will be talking about your issue in the grocery store, but it means that everyone in economic development circles is talking about it—or everyone in education, or in real estate.
- Track press coverage that mentions your organization. This is also inexact: Some of your best presswork might not include your organization at all (if it's about someone affected by the policies you want changed, for example). But if your ideas and organization are making it into the press, chances are that people are responding in some way.

POSTSCRIPT

Life After the Report

LIFE AFTER THE REPORT

How you proceed from here really depends on your organization's goals. If you're a service provider that just wanted to produce one report on a very important topic, congratulations. We hope that you were able to make a difference with your work and found this book helpful. If you're interested in continuing to do policy work—or if your group is in the business of regularly creating reports—we think you'll find that the process gets easier with practice, and that people will be more eager to see your work once you have a track record.

But we don't want to create the impression that getting reporters interested in your issue is the end of your efforts. It's just the beginning of a beautiful situation: the one in which everybody considers your opinion the most important one and your ideas the best. "We've become known as a place to call for ethnic press issues," says the Independant Press Association's Abby Scher. "People see our name in web searches and in Lexis-Nexis, so we continue to get press because of that. We got a call from someone doing a PBS documentary on the subject just last week."

That isn't to say that one report will put your name in the

Rolodex of every reporter in the city. Or that you can alter the debate with one study. "Changing public opinion is a very long process. It requires incredible redundancy and repetition. You want the idea to infiltrate their consciousness so they even end up thinking it was their idea to begin with," says Gail Nayowith. But once you've built a reputation, your group will be more and more able to be heard and have your ideas given thought.

Since so many different kinds of groups have a wide variety of expertise in getting their message out, we'll end this book without going into important communications issues like running a website or organizing a grassroots campaign. But please consider those issues. You've got good ideas: Don't forget to keep working to get them widely distributed. Whichever direction you take, we think that the facts, ideas, recommendations and anecdotes in your report will serve you well. *Best of luck!*